AF444953

World War I Trivia

500 Questions and Answers About Unforgettable Moments, Legendary Icons, and Lasting Impact

Welcome Aboard, Check Out This Limited-Time Free Bonus!

Ahoy, reader! Welcome to the Ahoy Publications family, and thanks for snagging a copy of this book! Since you've chosen to join us on this journey, we'd like to offer you something special.

Check out the link below for a FREE e-book filled with delightful facts about American History.

But that's not all - you'll also have access to our exclusive email list with even more free e-books and insider knowledge. Well, what are ye waiting for? Click the link below to join and set sail toward exciting adventures in American History.

Access your bonus here

https://ahoypublications.com/

Or, Scan the QR code!

Table of Contents

INTRODUCTION 1

CAUSES OF WORLD WAR I 2

OUTBREAK OF THE WAR 7

INVASION OF BELGIUM AND NEUTRALITY 11

BATTLE OF THE MARNE 16

SCHLIEFFEN PLAN/STRATEGY 20

RACE TO THE SEA 25

WARFARE AND BATTLES ON THE WESTERN FRONT 30

EASTERN FRONT BATTLES AND STRATEGIES 34

BALKANS THEATER 39

NAVAL WARFARE (BATTLE OF JUTLAND) 43

THE RUSSIAN REVOLUTION 47

AMERICAN ENTRY INTO THE WAR 51

THE ARMISTICE OF 1918 56

TREATY OF VERSAILLES 60

TECHNOLOGY USED IN WWI 65

PROPAGANDA IN WWI 69

HOME FRONTS DURING WWI 74

U-BOAT CAMPAIGNS AND BLOCKADES 79

BRITISH EMPIRE'S CONTRIBUTIONS 83

CREATION OF THE LEAGUE OF NATIONS 87

POST-WAR ECONOMIC CRISIS AND INFLATIONARY PRESSURES 92

IMPACT ON CIVILIAN POPULATIONS 97

ROLE OF WOMEN DURING WWI 103

COLONIALISM, AFTERMATH, AND NEW NATIONAL BORDERS.......... 107

MEDICAL ADVANCES, INTELLIGENCE GATHERING, AND ESPIONAGE DURING WWI.. 111

CONCLUSION 116

ANSWER KEY 117

CHECK OUT ANOTHER BOOK IN THE SERIES........................... 136

WELCOME ABOARD, CHECK OUT THIS LIMITED-TIME FREE BONUS! 137

Introduction

Welcome to the trivia book of World War I! In this book, you'll find all the answers you need about one of history's most important and devastating events.

The twenty-five chapters cover a wide range of topics, from the causes of WWI to the outbreak of war, technology used in WWI, propaganda during WWI, the home front during WWI, U-boat campaigns and blockades, and the role of women during WWI. This comprehensive book looks at World War I from every angle so that readers can gain insight into what happened during those tumultuous years.

Many underestimated how destructive this war would be and its lasting impact on our world today—from new political boundaries to technological advances. We'll explore some little-known facts about World War I, such as why Great Britain declared war against Germany when it was not directly threatened, how German strategy led to trench warfare along France's border with Belgium, and why American entry changed the entire balance of power.

We'll also look at some of the most famous battles, such as the Battle of the Marne, the Race to the Sea, and the Battle of Jutland. We'll see how World War I paved the way for significant political changes—like the creation of League Nations—but also left behind deep scars that were felt long after the armistice agreement was signed.

So, let's begin our journey through this trivia book about World War I! Get ready for an engaging exploration that reveals what happened during the years between 1914 and 1918.

Causes of World War I

In the early 1900s, Europe was a boiling pot of tension and competition between rival nations. Leaders were forming alliances, building their militaries, and struggling for control over natural resources—all of which created an environment in which war seemed inevitable. But what set off the chain of events that led to World War I? In our WWI trivia chapter on the causes of World War I, we'll explore this fascinating topic as we answer questions about Archduke Franz Ferdinand's assassination in Sarajevo, major powers' attempts at imperialism and militarism leading up to WWI, consequences during WWI's aftermath, and much more! Put your history knowledge to the test, and let's dive into exploring some important causes of the most devastating wars humankind has ever experienced!

1.   What was the immediate cause of World War I?
   a.   The assassination of Archduke Franz Ferdinand
   b.   The rise of militarism in Europe
   c.   Alliances between European nations
   d.   Nationalistic sentiment among Europeans

2.   How was Austrian Emperor Franz Joseph I related to Archduke Franz Ferdinand?
   a.   He was his father
   b.   He was his uncle
   c.   They were brothers
   d.   First cousin, twice removed

3. Which country declared war on Serbia following the assassination of Archduke Franz Ferdinand, triggering a series of events that would lead to the start of World War I?

   a. Austria-Hungary

   b. Germany

   c. Russia

   d. France

4. Which of the following events is regarded as a major factor of WWI?

   a. Formation of the Triple Entente

   b. Industrial Revolution

   c. Outbreak of Spanish flu

   d. Treaty of Versailles

5. What were some other underlying factors that led to World War I?

   a. Social inequalities

   b. Imperialism

   c. Militarism

   d. All the above

6. How did nationalism contribute to escalating tensions before WWI?

   a. It sparked protests in certain parts of Europe

   b. It caused different ethnic groups to unite and fight for independence

   c. It increased the competition between European nations

   d. All the above

7. What was one of the most significant consequences of World War I for society?

   a. The collapse of many monarchies in Europe

   b. The introduction of new technologies in warfare

   c. An increase in international trade

   d. Both a and b

8. How did militarism contribute to WWI?

   a. By encouraging an arms race among major powers

   b. By providing resources for military development

   c. By escalating tensions among European countries

   d. All the above

9. What was one of the main goals of imperialism during WWI?

   a. To gain control over natural resources

   b. To expand economic influence in other countries

   c. To spread religion and culture

   d. All the above

10. What were some consequences of industrialization leading up to WWI?

   a. An increase in global trade

   b. A rise in population growth

   c. Growing militarism in Europe

   d. All the above

11. What is an example of a secret alliance that contributed to the start of World War I?

   a. The Triple Alliance between Germany, Austria-Hungary, and Italy

   b. The St. Petersburg Treaty between Russia and France

   c. The Hague Convention on Naval Warfare between Britain and Japan

   d. Both a and b

12. Why did the Serbians reject Austria-Hungary's ultimatum in 1914?

   a. They feared it would lead to war with Germany

   b. They wanted full independence from their rulers

   c. They wanted control over Bosnia and Herzegovina

   d. They refused to allow Austrian officials into Serbia to participate in the judicial inquiry into the assassination of the archduke

13. **How did alliances contribute to escalating tensions before WWI?**
    a. They encouraged rivalries among different nations
    b. They protected weaker nations
    c. They made it easier for countries to go to war with each other
    d. All the above

14. **How did Britain's naval supremacy contribute to WWI?**
    a. By deterring other European powers from attacking
    b. By providing supplies and support for its allies
    c. By allowing it to maintain control over its colonies
    d. All the above

15. **How did imperialism effect international relations before World War I?**
    a. It created tensions between major European powers
    b. It encouraged cooperation among different nations
    c. It laid the groundwork for the Cold War
    d. It promoted free trade throughout Europe

16. **How did the assassination of Archduke Franz Ferdinand lead to WWI?**
    a. It sparked mass protests across Europe
    b. It led Austria-Hungary to declare war on Serbia
    c. It caused Serbia to declare war on Austria-Hungary
    d. It created tensions between Russia and France

17. **How did nationalism effect international relations before WWI?**
    a. It increased competition between European nations
    b. Greenland sought entry into the League of Nations
    c. It encouraged cooperation among different nations
    d. It promoted free trade across Europe

18. **What famous German once predicted that a major world war would erupt over "some damn silly thing in the Balkans?"**
   a. Werner Heisenberg
   b. Albert Einstein
   c. Otto von Bismarck
   d. None of the Above

19. **What was the Triple Entente?**
   a. An alliance between Germany, Austria-Hungary, and Italy during World War I
   b. An alliance between France, Russia, and Great Britain during World War I
   c. An alliance between Japan, the United States, and Italy during World War II
   d. An alliance between the United States, France, and Italy during World War II

20. **Who proposed closer ties between Britain, France, and Italy during WWI?**
   a. Kaiser Wilhelm II
   b. Gavrilo Princip
   c. Joseph Stalin
   d. Sir Edward Grey

Outbreak of the War

On the brink of the twentieth century, World War I began with a series of acts in Europe that would forever change the world. This chapter will highlight key events of WWI and their outcomes. From the "blank check" before the war even started to who was responsible for inciting action between Austria-Hungary and Serbia, test your knowledge about WWI's beginning and see how familiar you are with this tragedy that unfolded over four years.

21. Which country declared general mobilization on July 30, 1914?

a. Italy

c. United States

b. United Kingdom

d. Russia

22. What happened to Belgium after it refused to allow passage for invading German troops?

a. It became an ally with Germany

b. It was invaded by Germany

c. Its army surrendered

d. Luxembourg took control

23. Which country sent what is known as the "blank check," promising support for whatever action Austria-Hungary chose against Serbia before WWI?

a. France

c. United Kingdom

b. United States

d. Germany

24. On August 1, 1914, which country declared war on Russia?

    a. France

    b. United States

    c. United Kingdom

    d. Germany

25. Who was the leader of Germany during WWI?

    a. Kaiser Wilhelm II

    b. Adolf Hitler

    c. Otto von Bismarck

    d. Joseph Stalin

26. Which two European countries were the least involved in WWI?

    a. Italy and Germany

    b. Romania and Bulgaria

    c. Sweden and Portugal `

    d. Greece and Croatia

27. Why did Britain primarily enter WWI in the summer of 1914?

    a. To support Serbia against Austria-Hungary

    b. To support Belgium against German invasion

    c. To defend its colonial possessions

    d. All the above

28. What date did WWI start?

    a. July 28

    b. July 30

    c. August 1

    d. August 3

29. Which country was primarily responsible for inciting military action between Austria-Hungary and Serbia before WWI?

    a. The United Kingdom

    b. Russia

    c. Austria-Hungary

    d. None of the above

30. How many days after issuing an ultimatum to Serbia did Austro-Hungarian troops begin their attack?

    a. Two days

    b. Four days

    c. Five days

    d. Eight days

31. When did Germany declare war on France?

    a. August 3, 1914

    b. June 28, 1914

    c. July 28, 1914

    d. December 31, 1917

32. Who issued an ultimatum to Serbia as retaliation for its involvement in the assassination of Archduke Franz Ferdinand?

    a. Britain

    b. The Ottoman Empire

    c. United States

    d. Austria-Hungary

33. When did German troops first enter Luxembourg at the start of WWI?

    a. July 28

    b. July 30

    c. August 1

    d. August 3

34. How many countries were involved in declaring war by August 5, 1914?

    a. Six countries

    b. Seven countries

    c. Eight countries

    d. Nine countries

35. Who was responsible for mobilizing its army against Serbia at the start of WWI?

    a. Italy

    b. France

    c. Austria-Hungary

    d. Russia

36. On what date did Russia declare general mobilization at the start of WWI?

   a. July 28
   b. July 30
   c. August 1
   d. August 3

37. What was the result of Germany's invasion of Belgium?

   a. Belgium became an ally with Germany
   b. Belgium was invaded by Austria-Hungary
   c. None of the above
   d. Italy took control over Belgium

38. What did the German government promise to do if it faced war?

   a. Declare general mobilization
   b. Invade France
   c. Issue an ultimatum to Serbia
   d. Enter Luxembourg

39. What was the primary reason for France entering WWI in the summer of 1914?

   a. To support its allies against German aggression
   b. To defend its colonial possessions
   c. To prevent further spread and escalation of conflict
   d. All the above

40. How many days after Russia declared war on Germany did France declare war?

   a. Two days
   b. Four days
   c. Six days
   d. Eight days

Invasion of Belgium and Neutrality

When the Great War erupted, many countries scrambled to maintain neutrality so as not to be dragged into the devastating conflict. One small nation found itself severely tested when both Germany and France vied for control over it. Without warning, despite its status of neutrality, German troops crossed onto Belgian soil, threatening the lives and homes of innocent civilians while reviving a centuries-old international agreement that would change world history forever. In this chapter, we'll explore how one critical violation by Germany altered international relations with dramatic effect. We'll also examine questions such as, What were the consequences for violating Belgian neutrality? Why was Swiss-style neutrality significant during WWI? And which measures did Germany take after invading Belgium?

41.   **What year did Germany invade Belgium?**

    a.   1914

    b.   1915

    c.   1916

    d.   1917

42. **Why was the neutrality of Belgium important to both Germany and France?**

   a. It allowed for a safe passage between them during the war

   b. Both wanted access to its ports for military purposes

   c. The Belgian monarchy had close ties with each country's royal family

   d. It provided an essential buffer zone against attack from other powers

43. **What treaty prohibited any foreign power from violating Belgian neutrality?**

   a. The Treaty of Vienna (1815)

   b. The Schlieffen Plan

   c. The Treaty of London (1839)

   d. The Versailles Peace Agreement

44. **How long before invading did German troops occupy Luxembourg?**

   a. A few hours

   b. One day

   c. Two days

   d. One week

45. **How many divisions were in the German army that invaded Belgium on August 4, 1914?**

   a. Fifteen

   b. Twenty-five

   c. Thirty-four

   d. Seventy-five

46. **How did the German army enter Belgium on August 4?**

   a. By air

   b. Through Holland

   c. Crossing the border from Germany

   d. By sea

47. What happened to Belgian civilians when their homeland was invaded?

    a. They were forced into labor

    b. They were relocated to other countries

    c. They faced grave punishment

    d. They were allowed to stay in their homes

48. What measure taken by Germany made it difficult for Belgian citizens to flee the country during wartime?

    a. All borders were closed, and travel was restricted

    b. Passports were revoked

    c. Curfew was imposed

    d. Foreign passports were confiscated

49. How did Belgium respond when it found out about Germany's plans for invasion?

    a. Immediately mobilized its troops

    b. Requested help from France and Britain

    c. Asked all able-bodied men between 18 and 45 to join the army

    d. All the above

50. What was the consequence of Germany violating Belgian neutrality?

    a. It was invaded by Great Britain

    b. International condemnation

    c. Sanctions were imposed

    d. Both b and c

51. Where did many Belgians flee during World War I after their homeland was invaded?

    a. United States

    b. Mexico

    c. France

    d. Argentina

52. How long did it take for German troops to capture Belgium's major cities?

    a. Four days

    b. Six weeks

    c. Two months

    d. Three months

53. What happened in Belgium that caused outrage around the world and strengthened support for Allied forces?

    a. The execution of innocent civilians

    b. Destruction of civilian property

    c. Use of chemical weapons

    d. Abuse and torture of prisoners

54. What was the German military operation that led to the invasion of Belgium called?

    a. The Schlieffen Plan

    b. Operation Bad Nachbar

    c. Blitzkrieg Belgium

    d. The Charles Schultz Waltz

55. What did the Treaty of London (1839) guarantee?

    a. Belgium's neutrality

    b. German access to Belgian ports

    c. French control over the Congo

    d. British authority in India

56. Besides Belgium, what other country had a policy of neutrality during World War I?

    a. France

    b. Russia

    c. Italy

    d. The Netherlands

57. After invasion, what did Germany do to keep its hold on Belgium?

  a. Impose heavy taxes

  b. Set up military rule, destroy civilian property, and impose curfews

  c. Establish a puppet government

  d. Create concentration camps

58. How did German violation of Belgian neutrality affect the Belgian Congo during WWI?

  a. Forces in the Belgian Congo invaded German East Africa

  b. Belgian troops marched on Ethiopia

  c. Belgian colonists fled

  d. The Germans decided to seize the Belgian Congo for themselves

59. What led to Switzerland declaring its neutrality during WWI?

  a. The fall of the Ottoman Empire

  b. Increasing Russian aggression

  c. Pressure from Allied governments

  d. Fear of hostile invasion by major powers

60. What was the primary reason Belgium remained neutral throughout much of WWI?

  a. Its geographic location kept it safe from major invasions

  b. Its strong economy could withstand economic embargoes

  c. It had ties with both sides through trade agreements

  d. It had declared its neutrality publicly

Battle of the Marne

Immerse yourself in the thrilling story of one of the most decisive battles in world history—the Battle of the Marne. As tensions between Germany and France rose during WWI, both sides mobilized their troops to fight for dominance over Europe. On September 14, 1914, German forces crossed into French territory, marking the beginning of an epic conflict fought across hundreds of miles. Who would come out victorious? Were forces loyal to France or those backing up Germany? Brush up your knowledge of WWI military tactics as you go through this quiz about who riveted Europe with courage and valor during the Battle of the Marne!

61. **What marked the beginning of the First Battle of the Marne?**
    a. German air raids against Paris
    b. French mobilization to defend their homeland
    c. Germany's invasion of Belgium
    d. A British and French naval blockade on Germany

62. **Which nation initiated a retreat during the First Battle of the Marne?**
    a. France
    b. Britain
    c. Germany
    d. Italy

63. Where was the First Battle of the Marne fought?

    a. Italy

    b. Belgium

    c. France

    d. Germany

64. Where was most of the action taking place during this battle?

    a. The North Sea coast

    b. Western Front

    c. Eastern Front

    d. Mediterranean coast

65. Which statement best describes why the First Battle of the Marne happened?

    a. To gain control over nearby territories

    b. As part of revenge for WWI

    c. To establish a new government

    d. To prevent Germany from advancing

66. What was the result of the First Battle of the Marne?

    a. German victory

    b. French victory

    c. A draw

    d. British victory

67. How many soldiers fought in the First Battle of the Marne?

    a. 250,000

    b. One million

    c. 2.5 million

    d. Five million

68. Who were some of the notable military commanders on the Allied side during this battle?

    a. General Ferdinand Foch and General Joseph Joffre

    b. Emperor Francis I and Arthur Wellesley Duke of Wellington

    c. Kaiser Wilhelm II and Helmuth von Moltke

    d. Tsar Nicholas II and Otto Von Bismarck

69. When did fighting between both sides cease?
    a. September 12, 1914
    b. August 7, 1915
    c. July 15, 1916
    d. October 31, 1917

70. What was the name of the plan used by French and British forces during the First Battle of the Marne?
    a. Plan 17
    b. Schlieffen Plan
    c. Grand Offensive
    d. None of the above

71. Which event led to a decrease in German soldiers at the First Battle of the Marne?
    a. Fall of Paris
    b. Arrival of American troops
    c. Arrival of Russian troops on the Eastern Front
    d. Transfer of Austrian divisions

72. How many casualties were reported due to this battle on both sides combined?
    a. 250,000
    b. One million
    c. Three million
    d. 500,000

73. Who commanded the right flank for Germany during this battle?
    a. General Erich von Falkenhayn
    b. General Paul von Hindenburg
    c. Kaiser Wilhelm II
    d. General Alexander von Kluck

74. What did French taxis do to support the Allied forces during the First Battle of the Marne?
    a. Provided medical care for injured soldiers
    b. Transported troops and supplies to battlefronts
    c. Delivered food rations and ammunition
    d. Carried out reconnaissance missions

75. What did Parisian citizens do in response to rumors of German troops advancing?
    a. Started a riot
    b. Fled the city
    c. Took up arms and joined the fight
    d. Stayed indoors until instructed by their government

76. How many aircraft were used on both sides during this battle?
    a. None
    b. A few hundred
    c. Over a thousand
    d. Almost three thousand

77. When was the First Battle of the Marne fought?
    a. September 5-September 12, 1914
    b. July 15-September 11, 1918
    c. April 22-May 8, 1915
    d. November 10-December 18, 1916

78. Which army groups launched an offensive against Allied forces from behind at nightfall on September 9, 1914?
    a. The French Fifth Army Group and B Company
    b. The German Sixth and Seventh Army Group
    c. The British Eighth and Ninth Army Group
    d. The German First and Second armies

79. What was the key factor in allowing Allied forces to push back the Germans?
    a. Heavy artillery fire
    b. Superior air power
    c. More experienced commanders
    d. Better supply lines

80. Besides infantry, what type of military asset did both sides use during this battle?
    a. Zeppelins
    b. Submarines
    c. Tanks
    d. Aircraft

Schlieffen Plan/Strategy

World War I was an unprecedented global conflict during which a variety of strategies and tactics were employed. One such strategy was the Schlieffen Plan. With questions about who wrote it, when it was developed, and what its purpose was, among many others, this chapter will explore all aspects of the Schlieffen Plan from August 1914 until its eventual failure.

81.   **What was the Schlieffen Plan?**

    a.   A plan to attack Russia

    b.   An offensive of Germany and Austria-Hungary against Serbia in 1914

    c.   A strategic plan of the German Army for a fast, decisive victory over France and Russia

    d.   A military alliance between Italy, Britain, France, and Romania during WWI

82.   **When did Count Alfred von Schlieffen develop his strategy?**

    a.   1910

    b.   1905

    c.   1912

    d.   1915

83. Who wrote the successor to the original Schlieffen Plan after its failure at the Battle of the Marne in 1914?

    a. Kaiser Wilhelm II

    b. General Erich Ludendorff

    c. General Helmuth von Moltke

    d. Count Alfred Von Schlieffen

84. What was the main purpose of the Schlieffen Plan?

    a. To capture France with a swift attack

    b. To prevent Russia from mobilizing its forces

    c. To drive Britain off the continent

    d. To gain control of Belgium and the Netherlands

85. How long would it take to defeat France according to Count Alfred von Schlieffen's plan?

    a. Ten days

    b. One week

    c. Two weeks

    d. Six weeks

86. What event occurred in August 1914, leading German leaders to realize that the original Schlieffen Plan had failed?

    a. The Battle of the Marne

    b. World War I began

    c. The signing of the Treaty of Versailles

    d. Paris Peace Conference

87. Who replaced General Helmuth von Moltke as chief-of-staff after he cast aside some elements of Count Alfred von Schlieffen's strategy during WWI?

    a. Erich von Falkenhayn

    b. Paul von Hindenburg

    c. Kaiser Wilhelm II

    d. Archduke Franz Ferdinand

88. Which Belgian city did Germany attempt to take to gain access to France according to Count Alfred von Schlieffen's strategy?

   a. Liege

   b. Brussels

   c. Luxembourg

   d. Paris

89. Which country was excluded from attack by the Schlieffen Plan?

   a. Russia

   b. Britain

   c. Belgium

   d. Austria-Hungary

90. What did German commanders believe would eventually cause French forces to collapse and bring a quick end to their campaign in France?

   a. The Schlieffen Plan

   b. A strong defensive line

   c. Entrenched positions

   d. Support from Russia

91. What strategies did General Erich Ludendorff implement after the Schlieffen Plan's failure?

   a. He increased the military's size and strength

   b. He shifted focus away from Western Europe

   c. He changed the direction of invasion toward East Prussia

   d. He added an offensive against Serbia

92. When did Count Alfred von Schlieffen die?

   a. January 4, 1913

   b. May 9, 1922

   c. September 3, 1907

   d. April 1, 1933

93. Which French city did German forces attempt to capture in 1914 according to the Schlieffen Plan?

   a. Paris   c. Marseille

   b. Lyon   d. Verdun

94.   What war strategy prominently used by the Germans in WW2 was influenced by the Schlieffen Plan?

   a. Operation Paperclip
   b. Die Glocke
   c. Blitzkrieg
   d. Schlecht Mensch

95.   How long was the invasion of France supposed to take according to Count Alfred von Schlieffen's original plan?

   a. Ten days
   b. One week
   c. Two weeks
   d. Six weeks

96.   What did General Helmuth von Moltke do when he realized that the Schlieffen Plan had failed at the Battle of Marne in 1914?

   a. He assessed the situation and ordered a retreat
   b. He wrote an article criticizing Count Alfred Von Schlieffen's strategy
   c. He attempted to reinforce Germany's positions on both sides of France
   d. He shifted focus away from Western Europe and toward East Prussia

97.   Who wrote *Schlieffen Plan: Critique of a Myth*, which challenges the narrative that the plan's failure was due to the actions of Schlieffen's successor?

   a. Max Boot
   b. John Terraine
   c. Gerhard Ritter
   d. Hans Delbruck

98.   What was the main fault of the Schlieffen Plan according to historians?

   a. It underestimated France's military strength
   b. It overestimated Britain's naval power
   c. It failed to anticipate Russia's rapid mobilization
   d. Both a and c

99.   What was the code name for the Schlieffen Plan?

a.   Operation Barbarossa

b.   Operation Overlord

c.   Operation Red Dragon

d.   There was no code name

100.   What was the estimated percentage of troops Germany planned to deploy against Russia as part of its strategy for a two-front war outlined by the Schlieffen Plan?

a.   50 percent

b.   100 percent

c.   20 percent

d.   0 percent

Race to the Sea

As World War I entered its second month, the Allies and Central Powers engaged in a fierce battle for control of northern France and Belgium. This clash has become known as the Race to the Sea. In this race, both sides tried to outflank each other by advancing their armies toward the English Channel coast while struggling with difficult terrain, inclement weather conditions, and ever-changing frontlines. Achieving any significant advantage meant gaining ground swiftly, as time was essential. Thus, victory went to whichever side could gain territory faster than their opponent. Both sides employed many different strategies. Join us now as we investigate this chapter on WWI's Race to the Sea with questions about the objectives and challenges faced during this period of history!

101.   What was the Allies' objective in the Race to the Sea?

    a. To reach Berlin before enemy forces arrived

    b. To outflank and encircle German troops in France and Belgium

    c. To establish a defensive line from Switzerland to the North Sea Coast

    d. To gain control of key resources like coal, iron ore, and food supplies

102.   Who won the Race to the Sea?

    a. Germany   b. France

    a. Britain   c. Neither side won

103. **What were some challenges faced by both sides during the Race to the Sea?**

a. Difficult terrain and weather conditions

b. Strong enemy defenses

c. Constantly changing frontlines

d. All the above

104. **When did both sides stop their advances in the Flanders region as part of the Race to the Sea?**

a. September 23, 1914

b. October 12, 1914

c. November 22, 1914

d. December 16, 1914

105. **What were some strategies employed by both sides during the Race to the Sea?**

a. Rapid mobilization

b. Stalemate tactics

c. Flanking maneuvers

d. All the above

106. **What sea is the "Race to the Sea" referring to?**

a. Black Sea

b. North Sea

c. Mediterranean

d. None of the above

107. **What was the approximate total length of the Allies' uninterrupted defensive line that they established as part of the Race to Sea?**

a. 550-600 miles

b. 350-400 miles

c. 150-200 miles

d. 100-150 miles

108. **When did both sides start concentrating more on trench warfare rather than continuing with cavalry engagements?**

a. October 1914

b. November 1914

c. December 1914

d. January 1915

109. **What were the Allies' last attempts to protect their left wing during the Race to the Sea?**

   a. They shifted forces from the Western Front

   b. They moved troops from Italy and Austria-Hungary

   c. They brought in reinforcements from other colonies

   d. They set up a defensive line on the north coast

110. **The Race to the Sea ultimately resulted in what?**

   a. A trench warfare stalemate

   b. The German Army reaching the English Channel

   c. The French marching on Berlin

   d. The British securing the Netherlands

111. **After which stage did British commander Sir John French order his army for an offensive against Germans near the Ypres region?**

   a. First stage

   b. Second stage

   c. Third stage

   d. Fourth stage

112. **What was the objective of the Germans during the Race to the Sea?**

   a. Establishing an uninterrupted defensive line from Switzerland to the north coast

   b. Reaching Berlin before enemy forces arrived

   c. Gaining control of key resources like coal, iron ore, and food supplies

   d. Outflanking and encircling Allied troops in France and Belgium

113. **How did the Allies respond after they had lost their left wing in the Flanders region as part of the Race to Sea?**

   a. They shifted more troops to the Western Front

   b. They moved troops from Italy and Austria-Hungary

   c. They brought in reinforcements from other colonies

   d. They set up defensive lines on the English Channel coast

114.   Who established the shortest continuous defensive line during the Race to the Sea?

a.   British forces

b.   French forces

c.   German forces

d.   Belgian forces

115.   In what year did both sides stop their advances in the Belgium region as part of the Race to the Sea?

a.   1916

b.   1914

c.   1918

d.   1923

116.   After the Race to the Sea had ended, what did both sides do?

a.   Enter into a peace treaty

b.   Construct elaborate castle-styled fortresses every few miles

c.   Dig trenches and fortify their positions

d.   Hand out medals to the winners of the race

117.   Which sides fought each other in the Race to the Sea?

a.   Germany and France

b.   Britain and the Ottoman Empire

c.   Allied Powers and Central Powers

d.   Austria-Hungary and Russia

118.   Which of these locations were involved in the Race to the Sea?

a.   Ypres

b.   Aisne

c.   Somme

d.   All the above

119.   What battle took place around the same time that the Race to the Sea came to an end?

a.   Gallipoli Campaign

b.   First Battle of Ypres

c.   Dardanelles Campaign

d.   Battle of the Bulge

120. What event immediately preceded the start of the Race to the Sea?

    a. The Berlin Airlift

    b. The Battle of Verdun

    c. The First Battle of the Marne

    d. The Landing on the Moon

Warfare and Battles on the Western Front

At the beginning of World War I, major powers in Europe formed a Western Front to protect France and Great Britain from German soldiers. From 1915 to 1918, battles were fought between Allied teams, including forces from Russia, Canada, Italy, and the United States, against Germany's armies, which employed trench warfare tactics as their primary strategy. Thus began one of the most prolonged campaigns that would see hundreds of thousands of casualties among participants on all sides. Question yourself now on some facts from WWI's warfare operations along battlefronts such as Verdun, Somme, and Ypres. Let's begin!

121. **What was the Allies' main purpose of forming a Western Front during World War I?**

   a. To create an impregnable defensive line to protect France and Great Britain

   b. To launch surprise attacks on German forces

   c. To take control of foreign lands occupied by Germany

   d. None of the above

122. **How long did the Battle of Verdun last?**

   a. Six weeks

   b. Four months

   c. Ten months

   d. Eight months

123. Where was the first battle fought between French and German troops during WWI?

    a. The Somme

    b. Gallipoli

    c. Ypres

    d. Marne River Valley

124. Which Allied nation had its military command directly involved in operations along the Western Front from 1915 to 1918?

    a. United States

    b. Italy

    c. Russia

    d. Canada

125. Who commanded the British Expeditionary Force (BEF) in the Battle of Somme?

    a. Field Marshal Douglas Haig

    b. General Douglas Macarthur

    c. Sir John French

    d. General David Beatty

126. What was the primary strategy employed by German forces during WWI?

    a. Blitzkrieg

    b. Trench warfare

    c. Attrition warfare

    d. Guerrilla tactics

127. On what date did the Third Battle of Ypres begin?

    a. July 31, 1917

    b. April 22, 1915

    c. June 16, 1916

    d. August 20, 1918

128. How many miles long was the Western Front line at its greatest extent?

    a. 25 miles   c. 100 miles

    b. 50 miles   d. 440 miles

129. **When did the Germans first use poison gas on the Western Front?**

    a. The Battle of Verdun

    b. The Second Battle of Ypres

    c. The Battle of Constantinople

    d. None of the above

130. **What was the outcome of the Battle at Verdun?**

    a. German forces were successful and captured Verdun

    b. It ended in a stalemate with neither side gaining an advantage

    c. French forces emerged victorious and forced German troops to retreat

    d. Allied troops successfully managed to push back German advances

131. **What was the main way that German citizens were affected by warfare on the Western Front?**

    a. Direct combat

    b. Food shortages

    c. Allied threats of kidnapping

    d. None of the above

132. **What was the main objective of Allied forces during the Third Battle at Ypres?**

    a. To break through German lines

    b. To recapture strategic positions in Belgium

    c. To liberate occupied towns on the Belgian coast

    d. All the above

133. **When did the Second Battle at Ypres take place?**

    a. April 1915

    b. November 1916

    c. June 1917

    d. May 1918

134. **Which nation took part in major offensive operations along the Western Front from July to September 1918?**

    a. United Kingdom   c. Russia

    b. Italy   d. United States

135. What British invention saw action on the Western Front in a bid to break through the trenches?

    a. Hot air balloons

    b. Tanks

    c. Underground trains

    d. Steam powered robots

136. What was the total number of days fought in the Battle of Verdun?

    a. 300 days   c. 200 days

    b. 400 days   d. 100 days

137. Which one is not an event that occurred during a period known as "The Hundred Days Offensive" between August 8, 1918, and November 11, 1918?

    a. The Battle at Amiens

    b. The Battle of Valenciennes

    c. The Ypres-Les Offensive

    d. The invasion of Normandy

138. In what year did German forces launch a major offensive on the Western Front?

    a. 1915   c. 1917

    b. 1916   d. 1918

139. Which battle is known for Germany's heavy use of chemical weapons against Allied troops?

    a. Battle of Verdun

    b. Second Battle of Ypres

    c. First day on the Somme

    d. Third Battle of Ypres

140. What popular song was written to promote sending U.S. troops to the Western Front?

    a. "The Fixing to Die Rag"

    b. "I'll Fly Away"

    c. "Over There"

    d. None of the above

Eastern Front Battles and Strategies

Stretching from the Baltic Sea to the beautiful Black Sea, the WWI Eastern Front saw its fair share of battles and strategies between Europe's warring countries. Explore this part of the Great War in depth as we delve into trivia questions about various Eastern Front engagements that include Austria-Hungary and Germany, Hungary, Romania, and Russia. Discover who commanded which forces, who won important battles such as the Tannenberg and Brusilov Offensive, and how long it took German troops to occupy Warsaw. Have you ever wondered why Tsar Nicholas II resorted to the "Great Retreat" strategy for his military? Are you curious about what peace treaties were signed by Soviet leader Leon Trotsky? Test yourself with these intriguing trivia questions that travel back through time to find out more facts about World War I on the Eastern Front!

141. **What was the longest battle of World War I on the Eastern Front?**

    a. Battle of Tannenberg

    b. Battle of Verdun

    c. Brusilov Offensive

    d. Siege of Przemysl

142. In which year did Germany and Austria-Hungary launch a two-front offensive against Russia?

a. 1915

b. 1916

c. 1917

d. 1918

143. What were the "peace treaties" signed between Soviet leader Leon Trotsky and various European countries during 1917 and 1918?

a. Treaties of Brest-Litovsk

b. London Peace Accords

c. Versailles Treaty

d. Yalta Agreement

144. What were the goals of Tsar Nicholas II's "Great Retreat" in 1915?

a. To avoid encirclement, shorten the front lines, and buy time to resupply

b. To gain control over Eastern Europe

c. To force Germany to sign a peace treaty

d. To take back land lost to Austria-Hungary in previous battles

145. How did Romania end up going to war against Austria-Hungary on August 27, 1916?

a. Voluntarily declared war

b. Invaded by Austro-Hungarian troops

c. By signing an alliance with Russia

d. By joining the Triple Entente

146. What Russian city was renamed at the start of WWI because patriotic Russians felt it was too German sounding?

a. Moscow, which was renamed Stalingrad

b. St. Petersburg, which was changed to Petrograd

c. Archangel, which was renamed Perestroika

d. None of the above

147. Who were the allies that joined forces against Imperial Russia in 1914?

    a. Austria-Hungary, Bulgaria, and Turkey

    b. Britain, France, and Germany

    c. Austria-Hungary, Russia, and Serbia

    d. Britain, France and Italy

148. The Battle of Tannenberg was fought in what was then called "East Prussia." Today, this region is part of what country?

    a. Ukraine

    b. Poland

    c. Italy

    d. None of the above

149. What domestic shortage often contributed to defeat on the battlefield for the Russians?

    a. Lack of ammunition/munitions

    b. Lack of automobiles

    c. Butter shortage

    d. None of the above

150. What was the response of the Allied powers when Germany forced Russia to surrender?

    a. Allied forces attempted to intervene in Russian affairs

    b. Allied forces sent gifts to Tsar Nicholas

    c. Allied forces entered into immediate negotiations with Germany

    d. None of the above

151. How long did it take for German troops to occupy Warsaw after they launched an offensive against it in August 1915?

    a. Three days

    b. Two days

    c. Three months

    d. Three years

152. **What infamous adviser and insider of the Russian court was assassinated in December 1916, right at the height of the war?**

  a. Grigori Rasputin

  b. Mikhail Gorbachev

  c. Leon Trotsky

  d. Fyodor Dostoevsky

153. **After Russia was forced to withdraw from Poland and head further east, what Russian organization came together to aid in the evacuation of the wounded?**

  a. The Rasputin Red Guard

  b. Union of Zemstvos and Municipalities

  c. The Russian Rebels

  d. None of the above

154. **What Russian unit mutinied against its commanders in December 1916?**

  a. The Red Army

  b. The Fifty-first Kosack Brigade

  c. Rasputin's Honor Guard

  d. The Twentieth Siberian Rifle Regiment

155. **Who served as a commander of Russian forces during World War I on the Eastern Front?**

  a. General Erich von Falkenhayn

  b. General Erich Ludendorff

  c. General Aleksei Brusilov

  d. None of the above

156. **How did Austria-Hungary respond to Romania's declaration of war in 1916?**

  a. With a swift counterattack

  b. By signing peace treaties

  c. By negotiating with leaders from other countries

  d. By dropping an atomic bomb on Bucharest

157. Where did many of the battles take place on the Eastern Front during World War I?
   a. Poland and Romania
   b. Ukraine and Russia
   c. Russia and Austria-Hungary
   d. France and Belgium

158. What was the main aim of the Brusilov Offensive, launched by Russian forces in 1916?
   a. To relieve pressure on the Western Front
   b. To gain control over Eastern Europe
   c. To force Germany to sign a peace treaty
   d. To take back land lost to Austria-Hungary in previous battles

159. In what year was the Russian Empire forced out of Polish territory?
   a. 1919
   b. 1915
   c. 1917
   d. 1918

160. How did Germany respond to the Brusilov Offensive launched by Russia in 1916?
   a. They launched a counteroffensive
   b. They signed peace treaties with other countries
   c. They negotiated with Russian leaders
   d. They allied with Austria-Hungary

Balkans Theater

The Balkans theater of World War I was a site of battles and campaigns between many nations over several years. Austria-Hungary's declaration of war on Serbia triggered a conflict that soon involved each major European power. Throughout this tumultuous period, both sides launched assaults to gain ground, while various treaties were signed to bring peace. In this chapter, we look at some key facts from the Balkans theater—181 questions concerning who declared war, when and where important battles occurred during WWI, and their outcomes—so you can test your knowledge!

161. During World War I, which of these theaters of war was in the Balkans?

    a. Eastern Front

    b. Finisterre

    c. Suez Canal

    d. Western Europe

162. In what year did Austria-Hungary declare war on Serbia?

    a. 1914

    b. 1915

    c. 1916

    d. 1917

163. What is the name of the battle in which Austrian forces attempted to invade Serbia?

   a. Battle of Verdun

   b. Battle of Tannenberg

   c. Second Balkan War

   d. Battle of Cer

164. Who was responsible for leading Austria-Hungary's troops in the Balkans during World War I?

   a. Archduke Franz Ferdinand

   b. General Oskar Potiorek

   c. Wilhelm II

   d. Gavrilo Princip

165. What was one major event that occurred during the Serbian Campaign in 1915?

   a. The fall of Belgrade

   b. The signing of an armistice

   c. German occupation

   d. Austro-Hungarian victory

166. What famous American journalist found herself stuck behind enemy lines after visiting the warzone between Austria-Hungary and Serbia in the fall of 1914?

   a. Nellie Bly

   b. Whitney Houston

   c. Christiane Amanpour

   d. Ida B. Wells

167. What was a notable contribution of the Ottoman Empire to the Central Powers' war effort in the Balkans?

   a. The Salonika Campaign

   b. The Constantinople Campaign

   c. The Crete Campaign

   d. The Balkan Airdrop

168. What treaty was forced upon Romania during WWI?

a. The 1918 Treaty of Bucharest

b. The Treaty of Versailles

c. The Pax Romana

d. The Peace of Last Resort Treaty

169. In what year did Bulgaria enter World War I on the side of the Central Powers?

a. 1914

b. 1915

c. 1916

d. 1917

170. Where were Allied forces stationed during their occupation of Salonika between 1915 and 1918?

a. Greece

b. Serbia

c. Bulgaria

d. Albania

171. In what year did Greece enter World War I?

a. 1914

b. 1915

c. 1916

d. 1917

172. In what year did Bulgaria sign an armistice with the Allies, effectively ending its involvement in World War I?

a. 1918

b. 1919

c. 1920

d. 1921

173. Which famous leader was responsible for leading Allied forces during their occupation of Salonika between 1915 and 1918?

a. Erich Ludendorff

b. Archduke Franz Ferdinand

c. Eleftherios Venizelos

d. Gavrilo Princip

174. What is the name of one major battle that took place on Greece's Macedonian Front during WWI?

a. The 1917 Battle of Monastir

b. Battle of Verdun

c. Second Balkan War

d. Sarajevo Crisis

175. During World War I, which country declared war on the Ottoman Empire in 1914?

a. Russia

b. Romania

c. Bulgaria

d. Greece

176. When did the shelling and bombardment of Belgrade take place?

a. 1918

b. 1916

c. 1914

d. None of the above

177. What is the name of one major battle that took place on Romania's Transylvanian Front during WWI?

a. Battle of Tannenberg

b. Battle of Sellenberk

c. Battle of Verdun

d. Sarajevo Crisis

178. In a bid to rally Muslims in the Balkans and beyond, at the outset of the war, Ottoman leader Sultan Mehmed V declared what on/to Britain, France, and Russia?

a. Independence

b. Jihad

c. Bankruptcy

d. Principles of mutual respect and admiration

179. The alliance of what two historically antagonistic powers over a conflict in the Balkans is considered one of history's greatest ironies?

a. Austria-Hungary and the Ottoman Empire

b. Russia and France

c. Britain and the United States

d. Germany and Bulgaria

180. What was one major event that occurred during the Romanian Campaign in 1916?

a. The fall of Belgrade

b. The death of Tsar Nicholas

c. Battle of Transylvania

d. German chemical warfare

Naval Warfare (Battle of Jutland)

The Battle of Jutland was one of history's greatest naval engagements. Both nations fielded some of the most technologically advanced weapons in existence at that time, shaping modern naval warfare for generations to come. In this chapter of WWI trivia, we'll be taking a look back at this conflict's legacy as we explore questions related to military tactics employed by both sides, the technology used during combat, casualties suffered throughout mining operations, and more. Get ready to dive into a trove of questions regarding the Battle of Jutland as you test your knowledge on one of World War I's most notorious chapters. Pretty soon you will be itching to cry out "I sunk your battleship!"

181.   What year was the Battle of Jutland fought?

    a. 1914

    b. 1915

    c. 1916

    d. 1917

182.   Who were the opposing forces in the Battle of Jutland?

    a. British and German navies

    b. French and Canadian navies

    c. American and Australian navies

    d. Russian and Japanese navies

183. Where did this battle take place between British and German forces in 1916?

  a. North Sea

  b. English Channel

  c. Atlantic Ocean

  d. Mediterranean Sea

184. What was the primary weapon used by both sides in this battle?

  a. Tanks

  b. Submarines

  c. Aircraft

  d. Battleships

185. The British battlecruiser HMS *Indefatigable* was sunk during the Battle of Jutland after being hit by a shell in which part of the ship?

  a. The ammunition magazines

  b. The engine room

  c. The bridge

  d. The radar towers

186. What was the approximate total number of casualties as a result of this battle?

  a. 10,000

  b. 20,000

  c. 30,000

  d. 40,000

187. Which country led its fleet into the first clash with Germany's High Seas Fleet?

  a. Great Britain

  b. France

  c. Austria-Hungary

  d. Italy

188. What was the result of the battle?

  a. British victory

  b. German victory

  c. Both sides claimed victory

  d. Undetermined

189.	Who led Britain's Grand Fleet during this battle?

a.	Admiral David Beatty

b.	Admiral John Jellicoe

c.	Sir Winston Churchill

d.	Earl Jellicoe

190.	Who led the German High Seas Fleet in this naval engagement?

a.	Grand-Admiral Alfred von Tirpitz

b.	Admiral Reinhard Scheer

c.	Rear Admiral Franz Hipper

d.	Vice Admiral Heinrich Goette

191.	How many warships were sunk during this fight?

a.	Twenty-five

b.	Ten

c.	Fifteen

d.	Twenty

192.	What is another name for this major naval engagement between World War I combatants?

a.	Battle of Skagerrak

b.	Battle of Heligoland

c.	The Great Naval War

d.	The Longest Day

193.	Which country had more ships participating in the battle, Germany or Britain?

a.	Germany

b.	Great Britain

c.	Equal number

d.	Neither one

194.	Where is Jutland located?

a.	In Spain

b.	In Greenland and Canada

c.	In Denmark and northern Germany

d.	None of the above

195. How did both sides communicate during the battle?

    a. Flag signals

    b. Morse code

    c. Wireless telegraphy

    d. Both a and c

196. What is Jutland named after?

    a. The Norse god Jutlander

    b. A Germanic tribe called the "Jutes"

    c. A species of insect called "Jute bugs"

    d. None of the above

197. The German battleship SMS *Derfflinger* played a key role in the Battle of Jutland. What was its nickname among the Germans?

    a. Iron Fist

    b. Iron Dog

    c. Big Bertha

    d. Giant Killer

198. How many warships were involved on both sides combined in the Battle of Jutland?

    a. 145 warships

    b. 118 warships

    c. 100 warships

    d. 250 warships

199. What popular boardgame mimics and is inspired by massive naval engagements like the Battle of Jutland?

    a. *Battleship*   c. *Monopoly*

    b. *Life*   d. *Sorry*

200. What was the length of the battle in hours?

    a. Over seven hours

    b. Exactly twelve hours

    c. Just under seventeen hours

    d. Over twenty-four hours

The Russian Revolution

The Russian Revolution of 1917 was a pivotal moment in world history. The questions in this chapter explore the details and complexities of the wartime social and political reforms that unearthed Tsar Nicholas II's rule to give way to those led by Lenin and his revolutionary government. Test your knowledge with questions about key dates, groups, demands, leaders, and treaties—just to name a few!

201. **The Russian Revolution was a series of political and social reforms enacted in Russia during what year?**

    a. 1789

    b. 1891

    c. 1917

    d. 1923

202. **Which revolutionary group overthrew the provisional government to take power?**

    a. Socialist-Revolutionary Party

    b. Bolshevik Party

    c. Mensheviks

    d. Tzarist Autocracy

203. **What did Lenin's April Theses demand?**

    a. Nationalization of industry

    b. Abolition of private property

    c. Formation of workers' councils

    d. Creation of collective farms

204. Who led the Red Army during the civil war that followed the revolution?

a. Trotsky
b. Stalin
c. Lenin
d. Kerensky

205. What did the Treaty of Brest-Litovsk end in March 1918?

a. Russia's participation in WWI
b. World War I
c. Russian Civil War
d. Great Purge

206. Who was the last tsar of Russia before the revolution?

a. Nicholas II
b. Alexander III
c. Ivan IV
d. Peter I

207. After the 1917 Revolution, the Russians stopped fighting the Germans only to enter which other fight?

a. A civil war
b. The Winter War with Finland
c. The Russo-Japanese War
d. The Sino-China Border Conflict

208. In what month did elections begin for the Constituent Assembly that would create a new government after the Soviet Revolution?

a. January 1917
b. May 1917
c. October 1917
d. December 1916

209. Which revolutionary group wanted to limit power in an elected assembly rather than handing absolute power to one leader or party?

a. Bolsheviks
b. Mensheviks
c. Socialist Revolutionary Party
d. Tzarist Autocracy

210. What event marked the beginning of the February Revolution?

a. Bloody Sunday
b. October Manifesto
c. Lenin's April Theses
d. Petrograd Uprising

211. How did Tsar Nicholas II respond to the demands of protestors during World War I?

    a. He conceded to their demands

    b. He declared martial law

    c. He largely ignored and then repressed them

    d. He increased military conscription

212. Who was named prime minister after the abdication of Tsar Nicholas II and before Lenin took power?

    a. Alexander Kerensky

    b. Joseph Stalin

    c. Vladimir Lenin

    d. Mikhail Gorbachev

213. In what city did the most revolutionary activity take place in 1917?

    a. St. Petersburg (Petrograd)

    b. Moscow

    c. Kiev

    d. Yekaterinburg

214. Which group believed that socialism could only be achieved through gradual peaceful reforms instead of violent revolution?

    a. Bolsheviks

    b. Mensheviks

    c. Socialist Revolutionary Party

    d. Tzarist Autocracy

215. What event started the Russian Revolution?

    a. Bloody Sunday

    b. Lenin's April Theses

    c. Petrograd Uprising

    d. Bolshevik Coup (October Revolution)

216. Which of these was NOT one of the promises made by the Bolsheviks during their power campaign?

    a. Equality and freedom from oppression

    b. Land reform

    c. Private ownership of industry

    d. Free access to education

217. Who assassinated Grigori Rasputin, an influential advisor to Tsar Nicholas II, in December 1916?

    a. Alexandra Romanov

    b. Vladimir Lenin

    c. Felix Yusupov

    d. Joseph Stalin

218. How did many Russians feel about WWI when it began in 1914?

    a. Excited and hopeful

    b. Indifferent and apathetic

    c. Angry and resentful

    d. Enthusiastic and patriotic

219. During what period did Russia experience a famine due to the effects of WWI?

    a. 1914-1915

    b. 1916-1917

    c. 1918-1920

    d. 1921-1922

220. How did Lenin attempt to raise money for the Bolsheviks during WWI?

    a. Tax increases

    b. Selling off nationalized industries

    c. Printing more currency

    d. Robbing banks

American Entry into the War

The Great War of 1914–1918 touched the lives of people from all corners of the globe. As Europe stumbled into it, when did America join in? This chapter on American entry into World War I trivia will provide you with knowledge essential to understanding this important event in world history. We have questions ranging from President Wilson's initial response to German submarine warfare to who was appointed commander-in-chief when America entered World War I. Test your knowledge now!

221. **In what year did the United States enter World War I?**

    a. 1914

    b. 1915

    c. 1916

    d. 1917

222. **What was President Wilson's initial response to the outbreak of war in Europe?**

    a. He declared neutrality for the United States

    b. He immediately sent troops to fight alongside Britain and France against Germany and Austria-Hungary

    c. He imposed economic sanctions on all countries involved in the war

    d. He attempted to negotiate a peace agreement between all nations involved in the conflict

223. **Who were America's original allies during World War I?**

   a. France, Russia, Britain, and Italy

   b. Germany, Austria-Hungary, Bulgaria, and Turkey

   c. China, Japan, and India

   d. Britain, Canada, and Australia

224. **How did German submarine warfare threaten US interests?**

   a. By attacking US merchant vessels carrying supplies to Allied forces

   b. By blockading the US coast and preventing ships from entering or leaving

   c. By destroying American ports, thus cutting off access to supplies

   d. By launching air raids on major cities in the US

225. **What was President Wilson's initial response to German submarine warfare?**

   a. He declared war on Germany and its allies

   b. He imposed economic sanctions on all countries involved in the war

   c. He demanded the Germans stop targeting passenger ships and threatened to cut diplomatic ties

   d. He broke diplomatic relations with Germany

226. **What was President Wilson's primary reason for intervening militarily during World War I?**

   a. To protect America's interests and restore peace and freedom throughout Europe

   b. To prevent further bloodshed by ending hostilities between European nations

   c. To secure strategic resources for future use by American forces

   d. To gain control over valuable markets abroad

227. **What event is believed to have been the immediate cause of the United States' entry into World War I?**

   a. The sinking of the Lusitania by German U-boats

   b. The assassination of Archduke Franz Ferdinand

   c. The Zimmerman Telegram

   d. The signing of an alliance between Russia and France

228. **How did President Wilson initially respond to reports that Germany had declared war on Portugal?**

   a. He immediately sent troops to fight alongside Britain and France against Germany and Austria-Hungary

   b. He threatened military action against any U-boat that attacked an American ship

   c. He did not respond, maintaining neutrality for the United States

   d. He broke diplomatic relations with Berlin

229. **On April 2, 1917, what declaration was issued by Congress?**

   a. Declaration of war against the Central Powers

   b. Proclamation of neutrality toward all nations involved in WWI

   c. Declaration of independence from the League of Nations

   d. Joint resolution authorizing US participation in WWI

230. **What did the United States initially contribute to the Allied effort in World War I?**

   a. Money and supplies

   b. Troops and weapons

   c. Diplomatic support and economic sanctions

   d. Weapons, money, troops, intelligence gathering operations

231. **How many soldiers were deployed by the United States during World War I?**

   a. Five million

   b. Ten million

   c. Twenty million

   d. Forty million

232. Who was appointed as commander-in-chief of all American forces when America entered World War I?

    a. General John J. Pershing

    b. Admiral William S. Sims

    c. Colonel Theodore Roosevelt Jr.

    d. Lieutenant General George Marshall

233. What decision made at Versailles is considered one of President Wilson's greatest mistakes?

    a. Mandated reparations for Germany

    b. Creation of new nations out of former empires

    c. Forced disarmament on defeated countries

    d. Refusal to compromise with the Senate to ensure US membership in the League of Nations

234. What was the purpose of President Wilson's Fourteen Points plan?

    a. To provide for free trade between all nations involved in the war

    b. To ensure reparations would be paid to Allied countries

    c. To end alliances that had caused previous wars

    d. To create lasting peace and stability throughout Europe

235. When did America declare war against Austria-Hungary?

    a. April 6, 1917   c. June 28, 1919

    b. May 18, 1918   d. December 7, 1917

236. Who wrote "Over There," one of World War I's most iconic songs?

    a. George M. Cohan

    b. Irving Berlin

    c. Cole Porter

    d. Johnny Mercer

237. Why were American troops initially sent to France in 1917?

    a. To assist with the production of war supplies

    b. To provide support for Allied forces on the front lines

    c. To open new trade markets

    d. To help rebuild French infrastructure

238.   In 1916, President Woodrow Wilson ran on what WWI-related slogan?

a. He's going to send us Over There!

b. We've got to stop the Germans!

c. He kept us out of the war!

d. None of the above

239.   What was the US's ultimate goal in joining World War I?

a. To create an Allied victory over Germany and its allies

b. To gain control of strategic resources for future use by American forces

c. To ensure that all nations involved were held accountable for their actions

d. To establish a lasting peace and stability throughout Europe

240.   Who was President Wilson's Secretary of State during WWI?

a. Henry Stimson

b. Robert Lansing

c. Nelson Rockefeller

d. John Hay

The Armistice of 1918

The Armistice of 1918 (Compiègne) was a complex deal with several key elements and lasting effects that would shape the world as we know it today. In this chapter, you'll answer trivia questions related to the date of the armistice's signing, who was involved in the negotiations, consequences for refusal to comply with agreement terms, and more! Do you think you can piece together all the details of what happened during WWI's first official attempt at peace? Take this quiz to find out!

241.	**When was the armistice signed?**

    a.	October 22, 1918

    b.	November 11, 1917

    c.	November 11, 1918

    d.	December 10, 1918

242.	**Which entities signed the agreement?**

    a.	Germany and Austria-Hungary

    b.	The Allied Powers and Central Powers

    c.	France and Great Britain

    d.	All the above

243.	**Which country did not sign the armistice?**

    a.	Belgium

    b.	Italy

    c.	Austria

    d.	Netherlands

244.   What did the armistice mark for WWI?

a.   A victory for France

b.   A ceasefire

c.   An end to active hostilities

d.   A surrender by Germany

245.   What happened after the signing of the armistice?

a.   German troops stopped fighting

b.   French troops began mobilizing

c.   British forces declared victory

d.   All remaining countries agreed to peace terms

246.   How did most of President Woodrow Wilson's own political party—the Democrats—view the signing of the armistice?

a.   Fulfillment of Wilson's pledge to make the world safe for democracy

b.   A potential liability for the mid-term elections

c.   An embarrassing failure

d.   Controversial, disingenuous, and perhaps a bit dangerous

247.   Who had ultimate authority for the armistice?

a.   Marshal Ferdinand Foch

b.   King George V

c.   President Woodrow Wilson

d.   Emperor Wilhelm II

248.   What did the armistice stipulate?

a.   All territories to be returned to their original owners

b.   Open negotiations for peace

c.   Immediate surrender by Germany

d.   A cessation of hostilities and withdrawal from occupied territory

249.   Who was allowed into Paris after the signing of the armistice?

a.   Allied troops

b.   French citizens

c.   Both Allied and Central Powers troops

d.   Both a and b

250. **What prediction did Supreme Allied Commander; Marshal Ferdinand Foch make after the signing of the armistice?**

a. War would erupt again in twenty years

b. That long lasting peace had been secured

c. Hot war had just been replaced with a cold war

d. That the stock markets would crash

251. **Where were meetings held between both sides after signing the official armistice?**

a. Berlin, Germany

b. London, England

c. Paris, France

d. Washington D.C., United States

252. **What international body was formed as a result of this agreement?**

a. The Freemasons

b. NATO

c. The League of Nations

d. The United Nations

253. **What did the armistice state about prisoners of war?**

a. They would be released immediately

b. They must stay in prison until their country's surrender

c. Their release depended on negotiations between both sides

d. No provisions were made for them

254. **Who presided over the signing ceremony of the armistice?**

a. Kaiser Wilhelm II

b. President Woodrow Wilson

c. King George V

d. Marshal Foch

255. **According to the terms laid out by the armistice, which military forces had to withdraw from France and Belgium after it came into effect?**

a. Ethiopian troops

b. American troops

c. German troops

d. None of the above

256. Which Allied power did not sign the armistice because they had signed a previous one and were already out of the war?

    a. Russia

    b. France

    c. Britain

    d. Italy

257. What were the consequences for Germany if they did not accept the terms of the armistice?

    a. Potential Allied occupation of Germany

    b. A longer war with more casualties

    c. Even harsher terms

    d. All the above

258. Where was Adolf Hitler (a soldier during WW1) when the armistice was signed?

    a. At the negotiations table

    b. Drinking beer at a German pub

    c. He was a POW being held in France

    d. Recovering in a military hospital

259. How many articles were included in the armistice?

    a. Five

    b. Nine

    c. Eighteen

    d. Twenty-five

260. Who was responsible for supervising Germany's compliance with the armistice's terms?

    a. Marshal Foch

    b. Admiral Beatty

    c. General Pershing

    d. Prime Minister Lloyd George

Treaty of Versailles

As Germans watched Germany sign the treaty that ended World War I, many questions arose. How had it come to this? Who signed the Treaty of Versailles on behalf of Germany, and what kind of restrictions were put on German military forces? How much money did the country need to pay as reparations for damages caused by World War I, and under which article was blame placed on Germany for causing WWI? These are just a few of the questions addressed in this chapter about the Treaty of Versailles.

261. **Who signed the treaty on behalf of Germany?**

    a. Kaiser Wilhelm II

    b. Hermann Müller and Johannes Bell

    c. Vladimir Lenin

    d. Woodrow Wilson

262. **How much money did the treaty demand that Germany pay as reparations for damages caused by WWI?**

    a. One million deutschmarks

    b. 100 billion US dollars

    c. 132 billion gold marks

    d. 442 billion gold marks

263. What was established in 1919 to resolve disputes between states through peaceful means and thereby prevent another world war from breaking out?

a. United Nations

b. League of Nations

c. European Union

d. NATO

264. Which article section from the treaty imposed restrictions on German military forces?

a. Section I

b. Section X

c. Section V

d. Section XV

265. Which article from the treaty placed responsibility for WWI on Germany and its allies?

a. Article 16

b. Article 231

c. Article 43

d. Article 195

266. What was the name of the League of Nations' protocol that divided German colonies among Allied countries such as France, Britain, Belgium, Japan, and South Africa?

a. The Winners Take All System

b. The Mandate System

c. The European Union

d. The Territorialism System

267. When was the treaty legally binding?

a. June 28, 1919

b. January 10, 1920

c. May 7, 1921

d. April 11, 1923

268. **In what year did Germany pay off the reparations stipulated by the Treaty of Versailles?**

    a. 1933

    b. 1989

    c. 2020

    d. 2010

269. **How did most German Americans feel about the Treaty of Versailles?**

    a. It was unnecessarily punitive and unfairly placed too much blame on Germany

    b. They felt it served as a good course correction for Germany

    c. They insisted that their allegiance was with America and not Germany

    d. Since most German Americans were Democrats, they supported President Wilson

270. **What does Article 232 state?**

    a. That the Germans are wealthy beyond compare

    b. Allied recognition that Germany does not have the money to pay all reparations

    c. Victors take all

    d. None of the above

271. **What was the alternative name for Article 231 in the Treaty of Versailles?**

    a. The War Guilt Clause

    b. The Hunger Clause

    c. The Black Note

    d. Reparations Clause

272. **What did Japan—then part of the victorious Allies—get out of the treaty?**

    a. German possessions in China and the Pacific

    b. Lucrative trade deals with Germany

    c. An increase in tariffs

    d. Nothing at all

273.   Why was Italy dissatisfied with the Treaty of Versailles?

a. It felt sorry for the Germans

b. Italians felt that they did not receive enough territorial gains

c. It worried that the treaty could backfire

d. It was happy with the treaty

274.   Who chaired most sessions at the conference in which the treaty was negotiated?

a. Vittorio Orlando

b. Georges Clemenceau

c. David Lloyd George

d. Woodrow Wilson

275.   Which country refused to sign with other Allies when it came time to ratify peace terms in 1919?

a. France

b. Germany

c. Britain

d. United States

276.   What did the treaty require about Germany's military?

a. Germany was required to maintain an army of no greater than 100,000 soldiers

b. Germany was prohibited from having any armed forces

c. Germany was allowed to conscript troops for defensive purposes only

d. Germany must pay reparations for its military capabilities to be restored

277.   Why did the United States not sign the treaty?

a. President Wilson did not wish to offend German constituents

b. Because of political opposition to the League of Nations

c. Germany threatened war if it did so

d. Because of a disagreement with Italy

278. **What was the name of the German government that signed the treaty?**
    a. The Weimar Republic
    b. The Prussian Empire
    c. The Nazi Party
    d. Habsburg Monarchy

279. **How did the signing of the treaty affect Germany's size?**
    a. Germany had to hand over Alaska to the United States
    b. Germany was forced to cede territories in Europe and Asia
    c. Germany gained some new territories in Eastern Europe
    d. The treaty did not affect Germany's territorial boundaries

280. **What was the effect of the treaty on Germany's economy?**
    a. Germany's economy prospered due to increased trade with other countries
    b. The treaty caused an economic depression in Germany
    c. The treaty had no direct effect on German economics
    d. The treaty imposed heavy financial reparation payments that crippled its economy

Technology Used in WWI

World War I saw the emergence of a new type of heavy weaponry and the increased use of dangerous chemical substances and poison gases. As technology developed throughout the war, so did its usage in combat, with armies employing creative innovations on the battlefield to gain any advantage they could over their opponents. In this chapter, we'll look at some questions related to technological advances used during WWI. From aircraft to tanks that traversed muddy terrain, Europe had never seen anything like these modern machines! We'll explore who was responsible for introducing these innovative pieces of equipment, which countries initially employed them, and what benefits were offered by different models. So, let's dive right in—it's time for a roundup on World War I technology trivia!

281. What year were Sopwith Camel aircraft first used in World War I?

    a. 1914

    b. 1915

    c. 1916

    d. 1917

282. What type of poison gas was widely used during WWI?

    a. Phosgene gas

    b. Chlorine gas

    c. Sulfur dioxide gas

    d. Both a and b

283. What was the name of a German heavy bomber that saw action in WWI?

a. The Mousy Mouser

b. Mothball bomber

c. Gotha bomber

d. The Tiger II bomber

284. Who developed and introduced tanks to the battlefields for use by British forces at the Battle of Flers-Courcelette?

a. Henry Ford

b. Winston Churchill

c. Ernest Swinton

d. Rudolf Diesel

285. How were Zeppelins primarily utilized during WWI?

a. As observation aircraft

b. To deliver cargo

c. For bombing missions

d. As passenger transport

286. What was the most successful type of biplane used during WWI?

a. Sopwith Camel

b. Fokker D VII

c. SE5A

d. Albatros DIII

287. What type of aircraft offered more maneuverability and speed advantages than other planes in World War I?

a. SPAD XIII fighter plane

b. Bristol fighter plane

c. Avro 504K trainer

d. Handley Page 0/400 bomber plane

288. How did British forces use mustard gas in WWI?

a. Offensively against enemy troops

b. Defensively to protect military bases

c. To create smoke screens on battlefields

d. To poison food supplies for opposing armies

289. Which country used Zeppelins for aerial bombardment?

    a. Germany   c. Britain

    b. France   d. Italy

290. Who developed the tank-like landships that were used in the Battle of Somme?

    a. Robert Falcon Scott

    b. Winston Churchill

    c. Ernest Swinton

    d. Rudolf Diesel

291. About how many aircraft did Germany have at the outbreak of World War I?

    a. 1,500   c. 950

    b. 4,000   d. 230

292. What was the first fighter plane to feature synchronized machine guns that fired through its propeller blades?

    a. Sopwith Camel

    b. Fokker Eindecker

    c. Bleriot XI monoplane

    d. SPAD XIII

293. During WWI, what country salvaged/reverse engineered the British tank?

    a. Germany   c. Russia

    b. France   d. Japan

294. How did tanks help to break the deadlock of trench warfare during World War I?

    a. By allowing infantry and cavalry forces to advance more quickly

    b. By providing cover from enemy fire

    c. By helping soldiers cross no-man's-land faster

    d. All the above

295. What type of tank saw its debut on the Western Front in 1918?

    a. PAD X111

    b. Mark IV t

    c. A7V Sturmpanzerwagen

    d. Tiger II

296.   Who invented poison gas as part of his strategy for winning World War I?

    a. Alfred Nobel

    b. Fritz Haber

    c. Arthur Conan Doyle

    d. Charles Darwin

297.   How did the British use aircraft during World War I?

    a. Offensively against enemy troops

    b. Defensively to protect military bases

    c. To create smoke screens on battlefields

    d. All the above

298.   Who developed and introduced Zeppelins for warfare use?

    a. Henry Ford

    b. Ferdinand von Zeppelin

    c. Rudolf Diesel

    d. Ernest Swinton

299.   What type of aircraft was most responsible for the Allied victory in World War I?

    a. Sopwith Camel

    b. Fokker D VII

    c. SE5A

    d. Albatross DIII

300.   What weapon system allowed for unprecedented accuracy with long-range guns during WWI?

    a. Ballistics computers

    b. Recoil dampeners

    c. Rangefinders

    d. Gunsight scopes

Propaganda in WWI

Have you ever wondered about the power of propaganda during WWI? Have you considered how governments took steps to shape public opinion and control behavior? This chapter will provide an incredible look at some fascinating trivia related to this topic. Popular figures from Uncle Sam to Marianne were the product of propaganda efforts in wartime. This section reveals surprising insight into the matrix of propaganda used during one of history's most significant conflicts—WWI!

301. **What was the purpose of propaganda in WWI?**

    a. To rally public support for war efforts

    b. To promote patriotism and national pride

    c. To help win battles on the front lines

    d. All the above

302. **Which of these mediums were used to spread propaganda during WWI?**

    a. Posters, speeches, newspapers, and pamphlets

    b. Radio broadcasts, magazines, and movies

    c. Television shows, leaflets, and social media campaigns

    d. Art exhibitions, books, and plays

303. **How did governments use censorship as part of their propaganda tactics during WWI?**
    a. They suppressed news reports from enemy countries
    b. They censored any opinion deemed to be against government policy
    c. They prevented citizens from accessing certain materials that could affect morale
    d. All the above

304. **Who launched one of the most famous pieces of British propaganda in World War I with his painting titled "Your Country Needs You"?**
    a. Pablo Picasso
    b. Auguste Rodin
    c. John Singer Sargent
    d. Alfred Leete

305. **Which of the following countries was widely regarded as having one of the most successful propaganda campaigns during WWI?**
    a. France
    b. Germany
    c. Japan
    d. Canada

306. **Fringe political leader Emma Goldman produced propaganda condemning both sides of the war on behalf of what group?**
    a. Communists
    b. Anarchists
    c. Monarchists
    d. None of the above

307. **Who wrote the book *Propaganda* in 1928, which detailed how governments used propaganda during WWI to shape public opinion and behavior?**
    a. Edward Bernays
    b. Walter Lippmann
    c. Gustav Le Bon
    d. Karl Marx

308. **What tactics were used in German propaganda during WWI?**
   a. It played upon emotions
   b. It relied heavily on fear tactics
   c. It conveyed a sense of power and superiority
   d. All the above

309. **What did British propaganda do to sway public opinion against Germany in WWI?**
   a. Make the Germans look barbaric
   b. Suggest Germany had no honor
   c. Demonize its leaders
   d. All the above

310. **What ancient, warring, nomadic tribe were the Germans often referred to as in British propaganda during WWI?**
   a. Huns
   b. Indo Europeans
   c. Comanche
   d. Turks

311. **Which countries used iconic figures such as Uncle Sam and Marianne as part of their propaganda efforts during World War I?**
   a. Great Britain and France
   b. France and the United States
   c. Germany and Austria-Hungary
   d. Canada and Great Britain

312. **How did governments use propaganda to control public opinion during WWI?**
   a. By presenting only one side of the story
   b. By using catchphrases and slogans to influence emotions
   c. By censoring materials that could damage morale
   d. All the above

313. **What was the purpose of "war bonds," which were popularized by politicians, celebrities, and journalists in WWI as part of their propaganda efforts?**
   a. To raise funds for military supplies
   b. To encourage citizens to donate money toward war efforts
   c. To finance new weapons research
   d. All the above

314. Who wrote *The Great Illusion* in 1910, which argued that nations were wasting resources engaging in warfare when they should be cooperating economically instead?

    a. Norman Angell

    b. Alfred Mahan

    c. Emile Zola

    d. Theodore Roosevelt

315. What British prime minister declared in a speech on August 4, 1914, "The lamps are going out all over Europe. We shall not see them lit again in our lifetime"?

    a. Herbert Asquith

    b. Arthur Balfour

    c. David Lloyd George

    d. Winston Churchill

316. Who wrote the book *All Quiet on the Western Front*, based on both his experiences with war and wartime propaganda during World War I?

    a. Adolf Hitler

    b. Erich Maria Remarque

    c. Wilhelm II Kaiser

    d. Paul von Hindenburg

317. What were some techniques used by governments to control information about warfare during WWI?

    a. Censorship and misinformation campaigns

    b. Restricting access to news reports

    c. Limiting the number of journalists covering battles

    d. All the above

318. What was one of Germany's most popular propaganda slogans during WWI?

    a. "God punish England!"

    b. "Culture clash"

    c. "Germany is above everything!"

    d. "One nation, one empire, one leader"

319.   What was one of Britain's most popular pieces of wartime propaganda during WWI?

a.   "Your Country Needs You" poster

b.   "Keep Calm and Carry On" poster

c.   *The Great Illusion*

d.   "We Can Do It" poster

320.   What was a propaganda slogan used by the liberty bond campaign during WWI?

a.   Remember December

b.   Remember Belgium

c.   The Last One to France Is a Rotten Egg

d.   Four Minutes till Midnight

Home Fronts During WWI

The First World War was one of the most devastating conflicts in human history. It left millions dead and changed the fates of entire nations with its far-reaching impacts. But it is often forgotten that WWI also affected how countries mobilized their home fronts to join a fight unlike any before it. This chapter of WWI trivia will explore some unique technologies, policies, and campaigns used by governments around the world to manage their citizens' behavior during wartime, from America's liberty loan campaign to Britain's introduction of conscription in 1916. So, get ready for some interesting facts on home front mobilization during WWI—without giving away too many spoilers!

321.   What policy of President Woodrow Wilson significantly affected morale on the home front?

   a.   The expansion of segregation in the United States

   b.   The elimination of Taco Tuesday

   c.   The introduction of mandatory war bonds

   d.   The implementation of curfews in US cities

322.   During WWI, what did most soldiers do in their free time to keep up with news from home?

   a.   Read newspapers and magazines

   b.   Send postcards to family members

   c.   Listen to radio programs

   d.   Write and receive letters

323. What policy was put into place by President Woodrow Wilson that focused on providing food for civilians during WWI?

a. Rationing

b. Food control

c. Conservationism

d. Price fixing

324. Which country had some success with its War Industries Board, which regulated production, distribution, pricing systems, and labor conditions?

a. Germany

b. United States

c. Great Britain

d. France

325. "Save a loaf a week" was part of what home front effort during WWI?

a. The Meatloaf Share-a-thon

b. "Food Will Win the War" campaign

c. "Loafers Get Busy" campaign

d. Weekly National Food Drive

326. What was the primary purpose of "Victory Gardens" planted by civilians in World War I?

a. To provide fresh produce for civilians while freeing up commercial produce for soldiers

b. To raise money for war bonds

c. To beautify neighborhoods

d. To help boost morale and reduce stress

327. How many US citizens volunteered for military service during World War I?

a. Two million

b. Nine million

c. Four million

d. Six million

328. The liberty bond campaign used what kind of propaganda tactics?

a. Fear

b. Stereotypes

c. Patriotism

d. All the above

329. How did the National Defense Act impact civilians on the home front during WWI?

a. Established food rationing systems

b. Funded victory gardens

c. Allowed women into combat roles

d. Increased taxes and improved military preparedness

330. Who coined the phrase "Total War," which described warfare involving all aspects of civilian life?

a. Georges Clemenceau

b. Woodrow Wilson

c. Erich Ludendorff

d. Winston Churchill

331. What was the name of the US government agency created to manage military production during WWI?

a. War Industries Board

b. Office of Price Administration

c. Council of National Defense

d. Food and Fuel Control Board

332. What type of material shortages were seen on civilian home fronts in North America during WWI?

a. Food, metal, rubber, and textiles

b. Medicine and medical supplies

c. Vehicles, ammunition, and weapons

d. Electronics, jewelry, and luxury goods

333. Which industry saw an increase in employment opportunities due to wartime needs?

a. Astronomy

b. Agriculture

c. Plumbing

d. Banking

334. The introduction of conscription was one way that governments sought assistance on the home front, but what other methods were used?

a. Fundraising campaigns

b. Advertising initiatives

c. Recruiting drives

d. All the above

335. What did the US War Department absorb in 1918 to encourage women's participation on the home front?

a. Women's Army Auxiliary Corps

b. Women's Land Army

c. Victory Volunteer Corps

d. National Home Defense League

336. In what year was conscription introduced in Great Britain as part of their home front mobilization effort?

a. 1915

b. 1916

c. 1917

d. 1919

337. How did Americans on the home front show their patriotism during WWI?

a. Flying flags

b. Joining the military

c. Wearing red, white, and blue

d. All the above

338. What government agency was created to manage food production on the civilian home fronts in World War I?

a. U.S. Food Administration

b. Food Production Department

c. National Livestock Commission

d. Council of Agricultural Committees

339.   Initiatives under what government agency provided nutritional information and recipes to reduce public anxiety about food shortages during the war?

a. The US Food Administration

b. The Department of War

c. The US Department of Education

d. The Home Economics Education Initiative

340.   What campaign sought to encourage citizens on the home front to make a personal sacrifice by buying war bonds?

a. Selective Service Act

b. Liberty loan campaign

c. Home Front Initiative

d. Conservationism program

U-Boat Campaigns and Blockades

In the deadly game of WWI, U-boats were some of the most formidable weapons employed. The U-boat campaigns and blockades had a strategic impact on many fronts in World War I. Which country initiated a naval blockade against Germany? Which declared unrestricted submarine warfare? When did this campaign begin? How did Britain respond to German submarines roaming the North Sea? What types of vessels were used in these campaigns, and how many Allied ships were sunk as a result? Explore all these questions—and more—in this chapter on U-boat campaigns and blockades during WWI!

341. **What was the purpose of the U-boat campaigns and blockades during World War I?**

    a. To protect German borders

    b. To disrupt Allied supply lines

    c. To control enemy shipping routes

    d. All the above

342. **Which country initiated a naval blockade of Germany in World War I?**

    a. The United States

    b. Great Britain

    c. France

    d. Canada

343. **Which country declared unrestricted submarine warfare?**
   a. Great Britain
   b. France
   c. The United States
   d. Germany

344. **When did this country begin its unrestricted submarine warfare campaign against Britain?**
   a. February 1915
   b. August 1914
   c. March 1916
   d. April 1917

345. **During WWI, where did German U-boats engage the Russians?**
   a. In the Pacific
   b. In the Atlantic
   c. In the Baltic
   d. None of the above

346. **What was one consequence of the U-boat campaign?**
   a. Diplomatic goodwill for the world
   b. Free trade was readily available
   c. Increased diplomatic tension with the United States
   d. The Germans discovered a new species of aquatic life

347. **What types of vessels were used in U-boat campaigns?**
   a. Submarines
   b. Aircraft carriers
   c. Battleships
   d. Destroyers

348. **What was the purpose of unrestricted submarine warfare?**
   a. To damage enemy ships and prevent them from entering German waters
   b. To disrupt Allied supply lines
   c. To protect neutral shipping
   d. To sink merchant ships without warning

349. Who declared that submarines should be able to attack any ship, regardless of its nationality?

a. Kaiser Wilhelm II

b. Admiral Alfred von Tirpitz

c. Grand Admiral Karl Dönitz

d. Erich Raeder

350. During WWI, how did Britain respond to the threat posed by Germany's submarines?

a. It established an extensive naval blockade around its coastlines

b. Britain launched V2 rockets at German submarine bases

c. It built powerful battleships with bigger guns

d. It deployed minesweepers throughout European waters

351. How many U-boats were in service during WWI?

a. 500

b. 375

c. 100

d. 50

352. What was the primary goal of the British naval blockade against Germany during World War I?

a. To disrupt German trade and supply lines

b. To prevent food from entering German ports

c. To force Germany to surrender

d. All the above

353. How did U-boat campaigns cause many civilian casualties?

a. Through direct attacks on neutral shipping

b. Through indiscriminate shelling by battleships

c. By attacking merchant ships without warning

d. By targeting hospitals, schools, and other non-combatants

354. What year saw the height of the U-boat campaigns in WWI?

a. 1912   c. 1917

b. 1914   d. 1918

355. **What tactic was employed by U-boats to target merchant vessels?**

   a. Disguising as friendly ships

   b. Deploying mines in shipping lanes

   c. Torpedo attacks from underwater

   d. Bombing raids from aircraft

356. **How did Germany's U-boat blockade affect Britain during WWI?**

   a. It caused significant economic hardship

   b. It led to food shortages

   c. It cut off supplies needed for military operations

   d. It resulted in mass civilian casualties

357. **How many Allied ships were sunk by German submarines between 1914 and 1918?**

   a. 2,000

   b. 6,000

   c. 11,000

   d. 15,000

358. **What was the outcome of unrestricted submarine warfare?**

   a. Germany achieved naval supremacy

   b. Germany lost its naval advantage

   c. The Allied forces won the war

   d. The conflict ended in a stalemate

359. **What type of ships did submarines rely on to resupply their crews?**

   a. Merchant vessels

   b. Battleships

   c. Supply barges

   d. Submarine tenders

360. **Which country had the most effective blockade against Germany during World War I?**

   a. Britain

   b. France

   c. Italy

   d. The United States

British Empire's Contributions

During the war of 1914-1918, the British Empire and its colonies mobilized millions to join in the fight. From India to Australia and South Africa to Canada, these brave men fought with distinction, both in ground battles and naval engagements. This chapter of WWI trivia explores the contributions made by citizens within the British Empire during this global conflict. It examines questions about the number of battle deaths of Commonwealth soldiers, notable forces, and the funds expended for participation in this bitter struggle. Test your knowledge now!

361.   What part of the British Empire provided the most soldiers?

a. Kenya

b. Canada

c. Jamaica

d. India

362.   In which battle did more than 10,000 Indian soldiers die while fighting alongside Britain during WWI?

a. Battle of the Somme

b. Battle of Passchendaele

c. Battle of Kut

d. Battle of Gallipoli

363.   What Indian nationalist who would later advocate non-violence helped with the recruitment of Indian troops during World War I?

a. Benazir Bhuto

b. Siddarth Guatma

c. Mahatma Gandhi

d. Sudra Bose

364. What was the name given to Indian troops serving with Britain during WWI?

    a. The Imperial Army

    b. The Indian Corps

    c. The Sepoy Brigade

    d. The Great Army

365. As a British dominion, which of these countries was automatically expected to fight in WWI?

    a. United States

    b. Greenland

    c. Canada

    d. Mexico

366. How much money raised in Britain for war costs came from Canada during WWI?

    a. Two billion dollars

    b. One million dollars

    c. 500,000 dollars

    d. Twenty euros

367. What type of medal was awarded to members of British and Commonwealth forces who served in World War I?

    a. Victoria Cross

    b. Military Cross

    c. Order of the Garter

    d. Iron Cross

368. In which year did Australia become officially involved in WWI?

    a. 1915   c. 1917

    b. 1914   d. 1918

369. What was the name of the force formed by Indian troops that fought against German forces in Africa during WWI?

    a. African Legion

    b. African Brigade

    c. Indian Expeditionary Force

    d. Imperial Army

370.   How many ships from Australia's navy served in World War I?

   a. 50

   b. 100

   c. 150

   d. 37

371.   Who wrote the poem "For the Fallen," which became a national memorial to those lost during WWI?

   a. William Butler Yeats

   b. Rudyard Kipling

   c. Lawrence Binyon

   d. Robert Frost

372.   Which country provided more than 120,000 horses for British military service during WWI?

   a. India

   b. South Africa

   c. New Zealand

   d. Australia

373.   After WWI, which country gained control over former German colonies due to Britain's involvement in WWI?

   a. France

   b. United States

   c. Italy

   d. Australia

374.   Which country provided more than 5,000 fighter pilots for Britain's Royal Flying Corps during World War I?

   a. India

   b. Canada

   c. New Zealand

   d. Australia

375.   When did South Africa enter WWI?

   a. 1914

   b. 1915

   c. 1916

   d. 1917

376. India made a "special contribution" of how many pounds to the British war effort?

    a. One hundred million pounds

    b. Twenty million pounds

    c. Thirty million pounds

    d. Forty million pounds

377. What was the name of the association formed by Indian soldiers to promote their rights during WWI?

    a. The British Army Association

    b. The Commonwealth Treaty Union

    c. The Indian Rights League

    d. The Indian National Volunteer Corp

378. What was ANZAC?

    a. Australia National Zoo and Aquatic Committee

    b. A fuel derivative important for submarines

    c. A special medication used by colonial troops

    d. Australia and New Zealand Army Corps

379. In which battle did more than 4,000 Canadian soldiers die during WWI?

    a. Battle of Passchendaele

    b. Battle of Ypres

    c. Battle of Tannenberg

    d. Battle of Gallipoli

380. What former British colony became a crucial ally of Britain during WWI?

    a. Ukraine

    b. Ethiopia

    c. Japan

    d. The United States

Creation of the League of Nations

The Great War changed the face of history. Its reverberations left an impact on everything from politics to industry, leading to some of the most pivotal events in modern times. The League of Nations emerged from this tumultuous period. But between changing geopolitical dynamics and external political pressures, how successful was the league? Test your knowledge with these WWI trivia questions centered on the formation and implementation of one valiant attempt at establishing world peace: the League of Nations!

381.   **The League of Nations was formed in   .**

    a. 1914

    a. 1918

    b. 1920

    c. 1922

382.   **What was the main purpose of forming the league?**

    a. To establish a global peacekeeping force

    b. To prevent further wars and promote international cooperation

    c. To form alliances between major powers

    d. To provide economic sanctions against hostile nations

383. Who proposed creating an association based on collective security to prevent future war?

a. Woodrow Wilson

b. Winston Churchill

c. Vladimir Lenin

d. Gustav Stresemann

384. How many member states were there when the league was created in November 1920?

a. 50

b. 32

c. 42

d. 28

385. Who wrote the Covenant of the League of Nations, which became part of its charter?

a. Winston Churchill

b. Woodrow Wilson

c. Vladimir Lenin

d. Mustafa Kemal Ataturk

386. Who served as the first secretary general of the league?

a. Woodrow Wilson

b. Winston Churchill

c. Sir Eric Drummond

d. Gustav Stresemann

387. What was the main body of the league called?

a. The Council

b. The Supreme Court

c. The Assembly

d. The International Court of Justice

388. Which countries were not admitted into membership in 1920 when the league started its operations?

a. Germany, Russia, and Austria-Hungary

b. France and Italy

c. Britain and Japan

d. All eight nations mentioned above

389. How many votes did each member country have at meetings held by the league's Assembly?

a. One vote

b. Two votes

c. Three votes

d. Five votes

390. Who oversaw the implementation of treaties signed under the auspices of the league's covenant?

a. The Council

b. The Assembly

c. The International Court of Justice

d. All three mentioned above

391. What was the main source of income for the league during its early years?

a. Member nation contributions

b. Interest on loans

c. Taxation

d. Subscriptions to magazine publications

392. Patrons from which country provided financial assistance to the league when it needed funds and could not receive contributions from member nations?

a. United States

b. Soviet Union

c. Great Britain

d. Switzerland

393. What did the Mandates Commission do in 1924?

a. It developed plans for setting up colonies overseas

b. It monitored territories mandated by the league after WWI

c. It advised countries on how best to manage their economies

d. It proposed solutions to disputes between member states

394. What two League of Nations members became increasingly hostile to each other just a few years after joining?

a. Brazil and Mexico

b. Norway and Finland

c. United States and Canada

d. Japan and China

395. Which organization, created out of the league's initiative, aimed to promote international trade relations among members?

    a. Economic and Financial Organisation

    b. United Nations

    c. World Bank

    d. North Atlantic Treaty Organization

396. What did the Health Committee do under the League of Nations mandate?

    a. It monitored public health in member nations

    b. It provided medical aid to victims of disease outbreaks

    c. It researched diseases and their cures

    d. All the above

397. How many countries were members of the league at its peak in 1934?

    a. Forty-two

    b. Fifty-eight

    c. Sixty-eight

    d. Seventy-eight

398. Who was awarded the Nobel Peace Prize for his efforts toward creating and maintaining peace through the League of Nations?

    a. Woodrow Wilson

    b. Winston Churchill

    c. Gustav Stresemann

    d. Mustafa Kemal Ataturk

399. The Minorities Treaties drafted by the league aimed at which action?

    a. Establishing international law governing how minorities should be treated

    b. Promoting cooperation between different religious communities

    c. Providing financial support for education programs among minority groups

    d. Providing equal rights to all citizens regardless of their ethnic background

400.   What was the ultimate fate of the League of Nations?
    a. It disbanded in 1934
    b. It officially dissolved in 1946
    c. It developed into the European Union
    d. It merged with the International Labour Organization

Post-War Economic Crisis and Inflationary Pressures

The end of World War I opened up a new era of economic challenges and instability throughout Europe. After the war, many countries grappled with post-war economic crises caused by inflationary pressures, currency devaluation, reparations to former enemies, disruptive international trade agreements, political unrest, and social upheaval. In this chapter, we'll dive into these topics in more detail as we explore the various effects on European economies after WWI and how governments attempted to respond to them. Let's get started!

401. **How did the post-war economic crisis affect Germany?**

    a. It was forced to pay reparations that caused its currency to collapse

    b. Its economy experienced a period of growth and prosperity

    c. It defaulted on all its debt payments

    d. The government was overthrown by revolutionaries

402. **What impact did inflation have during the post-war period?**

    a. It improved living standards for many people in Europe

    b. It increased taxes and led to higher costs of goods and services

    c. It caused wages to remain stagnant while prices rose rapidly

    d. It weakened the government's ability to manage fiscal policy effectively

403. In what year did hyperinflation peak in Germany?

a. 1918

b. 1920

c. 1923

d. 1924

404. Which country experienced severe deflation during this period?

a. Italy

b. France

c. Austria

d. Britain

405. How much money had German citizens lost due to hyperinflation by November 1923?

a. Nearly 100 percent

b. 20 percent

c. 40 percent

d. 80 percent

406. How did the post-war economic crisis affect Austria?

a. Austria was forced to sell the crown jewels

b. Its economy experienced a period of growth and prosperity

c. The government was overthrown by revolutionaries

d. Austria faced inflation and economic depression

407. What effect did World War I have on global trade?

a. It decreased significantly due to tariffs, blockades, and other restrictions imposed during the war

b. It increased as countries sought new trading opportunities with one another

c. Both a and b

d. None of the above

408. What contributed most heavily to European inflation in the 1920s?

a. Rising prices for raw materials and manufactured goods

b. Decreasing wages for farm laborers

c. Increasing taxes on agricultural products

d. Increased debt and printing of money

409. **How did political instability contribute to Europe's post-WWI economic crisis?**

  a. Governments lacked resources necessary for recovery and reconstruction

  b. Governments had to borrow heavily from other countries

  c. Political unrest led to civil wars, which caused economic disruption

  d. All the above

410. **How did post-war inflation lead to a redistribution of wealth?**

  a. By increasing prices for everyday goods

  b. By decreasing wages relative to prices

  c. Both a and b

  d. None of the above

411. **What was one way governments attempted to address hyperinflation in Europe after WWI?**

  a. Implementing austerity measures such as budget cuts

  b. Increasing government spending on infrastructure projects

  c. By issuing calming sedatives

  d. Printing more money

412. **After World War I, what happened when traditional trade routes were disrupted?**

  a. Prices for raw materials decreased dramatically

  b. Countries became dependent on imports for essential goods and services

  c. Certain animals went extinct

  d. Global economic declined

413. **What did many European countries do to address post-war inflation?**

  a. They devalued their currencies

  b. They imposed price controls on essential goods and services

  c. Both a and b

  d. None of the above

414. **What were some consequences of deflation after World War I?**
   a. High unemployment due to lack of consumer spending
   b. Reduced wages and the inability to purchase basic needs
   c. Stagnation or decline in production levels due to decreased demand
   d. All the above

415. **Which of the following is NOT an effect of the post-war economic crisis and inflationary pressures?**
   a. Increase in unemployment
   b. Decrease in purchasing power
   c. Improved access to credit
   d. Increased investment opportunities

416. **What does a decrease in purchasing power mean?**
   a. People have more money to spend
   b. Prices remain low relative to income levels
   c. Goods are worth more than their original cost
   d. Consumers can buy less with same amount money

417. **Which country experienced one of the most severe bouts of hyperinflation during the interwar period?**
   a. France
   b. Germany
   c. United States
   d. Great Britain

418. **How did unstable economic conditions after WWI affect politics in Germany?**
   a. It radicalized them
   b. Most Germans became apolitical
   c. Public political speaking was band
   d. None of the above

419. **How did hyperinflation lead to political unrest in Europe during this period?**
   a. People had less disposable income due to rising prices for everyday goods
   b. The cost of living increased dramatically while wages remained stagnant
   c. Economic instability led people to feel powerless and frustrated with political leaders
   d. All the above

420. **What was one seemingly minor yet ultimately consequential effect of Germany's postwar economic downturn?**

a. An increase in wages made Germans more likely to support the government

b. Lower prices for goods caused a stampede at local stores (Germans like a good deal!)

c. Higher taxes on wealthy individuals led to protests from the rich

d. Cheap drinks and the political discourse of beer halls became popular (Consider the Beer Hall Putsch)

Impact on Civilian Populations

World War I left a lasting impact on the civilian populations of Europe. From the destruction of homes and infrastructure to wartime rationing, civilians faced hardship and deprivation in all areas of life. In this chapter, you will find questions pertaining specifically to World War I's effect on civilian populations, such as how it led to changes in public health standards across Europe and increased numbers of refugees fleeing violence. Prepare yourself for interesting insights into one of the darkest periods history has ever seen.

421.   **What effect did World War I have on civilian populations in Europe?**

    a. Increased poverty and hardship

    b. Improved quality of life for all citizens

    c. Reduced mortality rates from disease and starvation

    d. None of the above

422.   **How did the introduction of conscription during WWI affect civilians in many nations?**

    a. It allowed them to receive better opportunities for education and employment

    b. It caused a military draft among young men, leading to decreased labor availability

    c. It created more job prospects as wages rose due to increased demand for workers

    d. It resulted in an influx of money through taxation, allowing governments to provide better services

423. **In what ways did World War I cause civilian populations to suffer?**

   a. Destruction of homes and infrastructure

   b. Decreased availability of food, fuel, and medical supplies

   c. Increased taxes on citizens to finance war efforts

   d. All the above

424. **How did WWI contribute to the spread of Spanish influenza in 1918-1919?**

   a. It gave rise to a new strain of flu virus that was more contagious than its predecessors

   b. Troops returning home from abroad brought it with them

   c. The disruption caused by the war weakened people's immune systems, making them more susceptible

   d. It increased overcrowding among troops and civilians

425. **What factor(s) made civilians particularly vulnerable during World War I?**

   a. Limited access to healthcare services due to wartime rationing

   b. Lack of communication between governments and their citizens about safety measures

   c. The widespread use of chemical warfare tactics by both sides

   d. All the above

426. **What did the introduction of rationing during WWI lead to?**

   a. Improved living conditions for civilians in war-torn regions

   b. Reduced access to staple goods such as food and fuel

   c. Increased public health due to better nutrition among civilians

   d. A decrease in taxes on citizens, allowing them more disposable income

427. **Why were civilian populations particularly vulnerable at the end of World War I?**

a. They had limited resources with which to rebuild their homes and livelihoods

b. They faced discrimination from former enemies that had previously occupied their land

c. They were exposed to new diseases brought by returning troops

d. All the above

428. **How did WWI contribute to a decrease in agricultural production?**

a. By diverting resources from farming activities to military endeavors

b. By introducing new technologies that allowed for higher yields

c. By reducing access to labor due to conscription efforts

d. Both a and c

429. **How did World War I lead to an increase in child labor?**

a. By providing new opportunities for children to earn money

b. By allowing parents more time with their families

c. By reducing taxes on businesses that employed minors

d. Diverting manpower into the military, leaving fewer adults available for work

430. **How did World War I contribute to the spread of prostitution in Europe?**

a. By creating a need for cheap labor during wartime

b. By introducing new technologies that made it easier for women to enter the workforce

c. By forcing soldiers away from their families and creating a demand for sexual services

d. By introducing new laws that allowed women to enter the sex trade

431. **What effect did World War I have on public health in Europe?**

   a. It led to increased mortality rates due to disease and malnutrition

   b. It resulted in reduced access to healthcare services due to wartime rationing

   c. It caused an influx of refugees who brought with them new illnesses

   d. All the above

432. **How did WWI lead to changes in family structures among European civilian populations?**

   a. By allowing more married couples time together due to fewer demands for work

   b. By increasing poverty levels, forcing people into larger households

   c. By providing greater opportunities for education and employment

   d. Decreasing family size as men were away at war and women had to take on more responsibilities

433. **How did WWI contribute to a decrease in educational achievement across Europe?**

   a. By diverting resources away from schools to military endeavors

   b. By causing mass displacement, leading to overcrowding in educational institutions

   c. By introducing new technologies that made it easier for children to drop out of school

   d. By reducing taxation on businesses, allowing them more money with which to pay wages

434. **How did World War I lead to an increase in refugees?**

   a. By creating the need for people to flee violence and war-torn regions

   b. By providing incentives such as free travel or food rations

   c. By establishing sanctuary cities

   d. All the above

435. **What effect did WWI have on civilian populations living near combat zones?**

a.   Increased mortality rates due to disease and malnutrition

b.   Improved access to healthcare facilities

c.   Increased opportunities for employment due to military spending

d.   Both a and c

436. **Besides increased mortality rates, what effect did food shortages during WWI have on civilian populations?**

a.   Decreased birthrates due to malnutrition

b.   Family splits due to fighting over resources

c.   Improved nutrition among those who had access to food

d.   Both a and b

437. **How did World War I lead to a decrease in the number of small businesses?**

a.   By making it easier for large corporations to gain market share

b.   By diverting resources away from business owners and toward military endeavors

c.   By increasing taxes on businesses, leading them into financial hardship

d.   All the above

438. **How did WWI contribute to changes in public opinion about democracy?**

a.   By introducing new technologies that made it easier for dictators to gain power

b.   By creating the need for citizens to rally around their countries and fight against tyranny

c.   By providing an opportunity for different nations to collaborate in combating common enemies

d.   Both b and c

439.   How did WWI lead to changes in labor laws and regulations?

a. By introducing conscription, leading to decreased labor availability

b. By encouraging women into the workforce, allowing them more rights

c. By increasing wages due to increased demand for workers

d. All the above

440.   How many civilians died as a result of World War I?

a. 6-13 million

b. 15-17 million

c. 20-25 million

d. 25-30 million

Role of Women During WWI

WWI saw the emergence of a new role for women as active participants on and off the battlefield. As countries scrambled to mobilize their forces, they turned toward female workers and soldiers to fill gaps in labor shortages, boost morale, and prove dedication to the war effort. This chapter will explore the diverse roles held by women during WWI through trivia questions about some iconic figures, organizations, regulations, and landmark victories that pushed their presence forward on a global scale. Test your knowledge of when certain rights were granted or laws passed in various countries worldwide. You'll also be quizzed on more specific facts, such as the names of key leaders and volunteer corpses set up by courageous individuals seeking ways for females to get involved with the war efforts.

441. What was the first country to grant women the right to vote during WWI?

    a. Denmark

    b. France

    c. United Kingdom

    d. United States

442. During WWI, what iconic symbol began appearing on propaganda posters in North America?

    a. The Statue of Liberty

    b. Columbia

    c. Rosie the Riveter

    d. Marianne

443.   In which year were women allowed to enlist as nurses in a new branch of Britain's Royal Navy Reserve (RNR)?

a. 1902

b. 1915

c. 1917

d. 1919

444.   How many U-boats did German women pilots fly during WWI?

a. Zero

b. Two

c. Four

d. Six

445.   Which of the following was an international humanitarian organization women often participated in during World War I?

a. The Red Cross

b. The Hospitallers

c. The Green Crescent

d. The Traveling Medicine Show

446.   In which year did Britain create a woman-only branch of their military forces, called "Women's Royal Naval Service"?

a. 1917

b. 1918

c. 1920

d. 1922

447.   During WWI, what sector were most British women working in?

a. Factory work

b. Nursing

c. Domestic service

d. Agriculture

448.   How many African American nurses served as part of the United States Army Nurse Corps during WWI?

a. 18   c. 73

b. 30   d. 200

449. In what year did the Women's Land Army of America (WLA) begin recruiting women to work in agriculture during WWI?

a. 1916

b. 1917

c. 1918

d. 1919

450. What influential book was penned by French feminist Juliette Adam during WWI?

a. *Johnny Got His Gun*

b. *The Grapes of Wrath*

c. *The Schemes of the Kaiser*

d. *The George Sand Chronicles*

451. About how many American nurses served overseas with Base Hospital No. 45, an all-female hospital unit, during WWI?

a. 100

b. 150

c. 250

d. 300

452. What was the name of the first American woman to enlist in the marine corps in WWI?

a. Opha May Johnson

b. Mary Edwards Walker

c. Elizabeth Barnes

d. Margaret Corbin

453. During WWI, what was the primary role of women in Germany's military forces?

a. Supply and logistics

b. Medical support

c. Combat roles

d. Intelligence operations

454. In 1920, which country passed a law that allowed women to become lawyers for the first time?

a. France

b. United Kingdom

c. United States

d. Canada

455. Who was Russia's first (and fairly famous) female pilot during WWI?

    a. Yuri Gagarin

    b. Princess Evgeniya Shakhovskaya

    c. Baba Vanga

    d. Natasha Rasputina

456. About what percentage of American women worked outside their homes for wages during WWI?

    a. 10 percent   c. 40 percent

    b. 25 percent   d. 75 percent

457. In which year did Britain pass the Representation of the People Act, granting some women over thirty years old the right to vote for the first time?

    a. 1907   c. 1918

    b. 1915   d. 1928

458. Which organization was founded by British suffragettes Christabel and Emmeline Pankhurst in 1903 to fight for "Votes For Women"?

    a. The National Women's Army Corps

    b. The Red Cross

    c. The Women's Social and Political Union

    d. La Femme Ambulance Volontaire (FAV)

459. About how many American women served in the United States Navy during WWI?

    a. Over 3,000

    b. Over 10,000

    c. Over 20,000

    d. Over 30,000

460. What was the name of the female chemist in Germany who objected to the use of chemical weapons during WWI?

    a. Anna Tumarkin

    b. Maria von Wedemeyer

    c. Clara Immerwahr

    d. Elsbeth Schragmüller

Colonialism, Aftermath, and New National Borders

The conclusion of World War I saw a significant shift in the political order. Former territories emerged as independent countries formed by the redrawing of boundaries that had been obscured during European colonialism. In this chapter, we'll explore some of these new nations and examine how new territorial borders emerged. Discover which former colonies gained independence from their masters after WWI, from Yugoslavia to India and Pakistan, through mandates imposed by the League of Nations. Are you ready to become an expert on colonialism, the aftermath of WWI, and new national borders? Let's find out!

461. **Following WWI, which country became part of Yugoslavia?**

    a. Lichtenstein

    b. Lithuania

    c. Serbia

    d. Estonia

462. **What African country remained uncolonized post-WWI?**

    a. Sudan

    b. Ethiopia

    c. Somalia

    d. Zimbabwe

463. **After WWI, what treaty established an independent Poland for the first time since 1795?**

    a. Treaty of Brest Litovsk

    b. Trianon Peace Conference

    c. Paris Peace Conference

    d. Treaty of Versailles

464. At the end of WWI, which country surrendered its colonial territories to Britain and France?

    a. Egypt

    b. Germany

    c. Italy

    d. Austria

465. **How was the U.S. overseas territory of the Philippines affected by World War I?**

    a. There was an increased push toward self-determination and independence

    b. It was flooded with German refugees

    c. Spain began issuing demands for the U.S. to return its colony

    d. None of the above

466. **How did the League of Nations help to create new national borders in Europe after WWI?**

    a. By providing economic aid

    b. By creating demilitarized zones

    c. By issuing mandates for territories formerly controlled by defeated powers

    d. All the above

467. **In what year did Iraq gain independence from Britain following WWI?**

    a. 1914

    b. 1919

    c. 1923

    d. 1932

468. What was the name of the treaty that ended British rule over India and Pakistan in 1947?

    a. Potsdam Agreement

    b. Treaty of Versailles

    c. Partition Plan

    d. Indian Independence Act

469. What was the secret agreement between France and Britain to divide up the Ottoman Empire called?

    a. Sykes-Picot Agreement

    b. The Latter-Day Crusade

    c. The Armageddon Protocol

    d. Ordo Templi Orientis

470. After WWI, what did the League of Nations mandate for territories formerly controlled by defeated powers?

    a. They were to be divided among victorious nations

    b. They were to eventually become independent countries

    c. They were to form an international organization

    d. All the above

471. In what year was the Ottoman Empire dissolved following World War I?

    a. 1913

    b. 1918

    c. 1922

    d. 1939

472. In 1921, what German colonies in Africa became mandated by the League of Nations following WWI?

    a. Zimbabwe, Ethiopia, and Algeria

    b. Kenya, Somalia, and Uganda

    c. Mali, Sudan, and Chad

    d. Tanganyika, Togoland, and Cameroon

473. In what year did the League of Nations mandate Syria to France following WWI?

    a. 1914   c. 1922

    b. 1919   d. 1932

474. **What country declared independence from Russia in 1918?**

    a. Estonia   c. Lithuania

    b. Latvia   d. All the above

475. **How many Middle East countries were created after World War I because of the groundwork laid by the Sykes-Picot Agreement?**

    a. Five   c. Fifteen

    b. Ten   d. Twenty

476. **Which European country gained former Ottoman territories following WWI with the Treaty of Lausanne?**

    a. Italy   c. Bulgaria

    b. Greece   d. Romania

477. **The former heartland of the Ottoman Empire became what country?**

    a. Syria   c. Jordan

    b. Lebanon   d. Turkey

478. **In what year did the League of Nations mandate Palestine to Britain following WWI?**

    a. 1914   c. 1922

    b. 1919   d. 1932

479. **How did the League of Nations help to create new national borders in Asia after WWI?**

    a. By providing economic aid

    b. By creating demilitarized zones

    c. By issuing mandates for territories formerly controlled by defeated powers

    d. All the above

480. **Which two countries carved up German colonies in the Pacific Ocean at the end of World War I?**

    a. Portugal and Spain

    b. France and Belgium

    c. Britain and Russia

    d. Japan and Britain (through Australia/New Zealand)

Medical Advances, Intelligence Gathering, and Espionage during WWI

The First World War brought advanced technology, medical breakthroughs, and new forms of espionage as armies on both sides vied for supremacy in a four-year-long battle of attrition that left millions dead and wounded. This chapter explores some of the medical advances, intelligence techniques, and clandestine activities undertaken during WWI by examining trivia questions related to these topics. Learn about the ciphers and code-breaking that revolutionized intelligence gathering, artificial limb design that allowed injured soldiers to return home from the battlefield, advances in X-ray imaging that provided lifesaving diagnoses, and who developed effective gas masks—just by reading each question!

481.   What technique did British military intelligence use to intercept and decode German messages during WWI?

   a.   Ciphers

   b.   Cryptography

   c.   Codebreaking

   d.   Espionage

482. How long was a U-boat able to remain underwater before needing to surface during WWI?

a. Thirty minutes

c. Five hours

b. One hour

d. Two hours

483. Who invented X-ray technology, which revolutionized medical imaging during WWI?

a. Wilhelm Röntgen

b. Marie Curie

c. Pierre Curie

d. Henri Becquerel

484. How was computing technology used for military intelligence during WWI?

a. Artillery and anti-aircraft fire control

b. To surf the net

c. To calculate surface to air missile coordinates

d. To store data on chemical weapons

485. What medical advancement allowed soldiers to be transported safely and quickly from the battlefield during WWI?

a. Motorized ambulance transport

b. Antibiotic drugs

c. Anesthesia

d. Blood transfusions

486. During what year did Britain use aerial photography for intelligence-gathering purposes for the first time?

a. 1914

c. 1916

b. 1915

d. 1917

487. Who founded an organization called "The American Committee for Devastated France" to provide aid to French war victims during WWI?

a. Herbert Hoover

b. Henry Ford

c. Anne Morgan

d. Andrew Carnegie

488. Which German spy was executed by firing squad at Britain's Tower of London in November 1914?

    a. Carl Hans Lody   c. Johann Tetzel

    b. Hans Holzel   d. Johann Holzel

489. Which technique did British intelligence use to detect German U-boats during WWI?

    a. Radar   c. Radio signals

    b. Sonar   d. Morse code

490. Who invented a new type of gas mask that was used by British soldiers in WWI?

    a. John Scott Haldane

    b. Ernest Rutherford

    c. Marie Curie

    d. Frederick Soddy

491. What is the name of the British codebreaking operation that was used to decipher German messages during WWI?

    a. Room 40

    b. The Enigma Machine

    c. Bletchley Park

    d. Colossus

492. How did Germany use espionage and intelligence-gathering techniques to gain an advantage over its enemies during WWI?

    a. By infiltrating enemy lines

    b. By intercepting communications

    c. By planting spies inside government organizations

    d. All the above

493. Which weapon revolutionized trench warfare by allowing for movement between trenches during WWI?

    a. Machine guns

    b. Flamethrowers

    c. Tanks

    d. Submarines

494. For what reason were German Americans held at Fort Oglethorpe in Georgia from 1917 to 1920?

    a. To spread awareness of German culture

    b. Fear of espionage

    c. For military training

    d. To quarantine those affected by the Spanish flu

495. What medical procedure significantly improved during WWI?

    a. Skin grafts

    b. Cancer treatments

    c. Heart transplants

    d. Liposuction

496. Which invention revolutionized battlefield communication during World War I?

    a. Radio   c. Telegraph

    b. Telephone   d. Morse code

497. What was one way intelligence-gathering techniques helped the French and British forces gain an advantage during WWI?

    a. Through the use of signals intelligence

    b. By creating body doubles of German political figures

    c. By creating conspiracy theories about the End Times among the Ottomans

    d. None of the above

498. What malady of the trenches necessitated swift medical intervention?

    a. Trench foot

    b. The Spanish flu

    c. Malaria

    d. Big foot

499. What was the first artificial limb designed for a WWI veteran?

    a. A PROSTHETIC arm

    b. A prosthetic leg

    c. An artificial eye

    d. A mechanical hand

500. What huge aircraft did the Germans use for both bombing and intelligence gathering?

a. B-52 bombers

b. Zeppelins

c. V2 rockets

d. Military gliders

Conclusion

This trivia book has taken us through the causes, battles, and strategies of World War I, as well as its aftermath. We've explored technology used in WWI, such as submarines and airplanes; propaganda campaigns to mobilize civilian populations around the world; U-boat campaigns against merchant ships; contributions made by the British Empire on a global scale during wartime; and the creation of new national borders after colonial powers were weakened or defeated.

In addition, we've looked at medical advances that were developed due to wartime conditions, intelligence gathering efforts and espionage activities by both sides, and how women played a part in war efforts worldwide.

In reflecting on our journey through this World War I trivia book, it's easy to see just how much changed throughout Europe (and beyond) between 1914 and 1918, from technological advancements shaped by the necessity of warfare to societal shifts. It's no wonder why "The Great War" remains one of the most studied wars in history.

Answer Key

Causes of World War I

1. A. The assassination of Archduke Franz Ferdinand
2. b. He was his uncle
3. a. Austria-Hungary
4. a. Formation of the Triple Entente
5. d. All the above
6. d. All the above
7. d. Both a and b
8. d. All the above
9. d. All the above
10. d. All the above
11. a. The Triple Alliance between Germany, Austria-Hungary, and Italy
12. d. They refused to allow Austrian officials into Serbia to participate in the judicial inquiry into the assassination of the archduke
13. d. All the above
14. d. All the above
15. a. It created tensions between major European powers
16. b. It led Austria-Hungary to declare war on Serbia
17. a. It increased competition between European nations

18.   c. Otto von Bismarck

19.   b. An alliance between France, Russia, and Great Britain during World War I

20.   d. Sir Edward Grey

Outbreak of the War

21.   d. Russia

22.   b. It was invaded by Germany

23.   d. Germany

24.   d. Germany

25.   a. Kaiser Wilhelm II

26.   c. Sweden and Portugal

27.   b. To support Belgium against German invasion

28.   a. July 28

29.   c. Austria-Hungary

30.   c. Five days

31.   a. August 3, 1914

32.   d. Austria-Hungary

33.   c. August 1

34.   c. Eight countries

35.   c. Austria-Hungary

36.   b. July 30

37.   c. None of the above

38.   a. Declare general mobilization

39.   a. To support its allies against German aggression

40.   a. Two days

Invasion of Belgium and Neutrality

41.   a. 1914

42.   d. It provided an essential buffer zone against attack from other powers

43.   c. The Treaty of London (1839)

44.   b. One day

45.   c. Thirty-four

46.   c. Crossing the border from Germany

47.   a. They were forced into labor

48.   a. All borders were closed, and travel was restricted

49.   d. All the above

50.   a. Both b and c

51.   c. France

52.   c. Two months

53.   a. The execution of innocent civilians

54.   a. The Schlieffen Plan

55.   a. Belgium's neutrality

56.   d. The Netherlands

57.   b. Destroy civilian property and impose curfews

58.   a. Forces in the Belgian Congo invaded German East Africa

59.   d. Fear of hostile invasion by major powers

60.   d. It had declared its neutrality publicly

Battle of the Marne

61.   b. French mobilization to defend their homeland

62.   c. Germany

63.   c. France

64.   b. Western Front

65.   d. To prevent Germany from advancing

66.   b. French victory

67.   c. 2.5 million

68.   a. General Ferdinand Foch and General Joseph Joffre

69.   a. September 12, 1914

70.   d. None of the above

71.   c. Arrival of Russian troops on the Eastern Front

72.   d. 500,000

73.   d. General Alexander von Kluck

74.   b. Transported troops and supplies to battlefronts

75.   b. Fled the city

76.   b. A few hundred

77.   a. September 5–September 12, 1914

78.   b. The German First and Second armies

79.   d. Better supply lines

80.   d. Aircraft

Schlieffen Plan/Strategy

81.   c. A strategic plan of the German Army for a fast, decisive victory over France and Russia

82.   b. 1905

83.   b. General Helmuth von Moltke

84.   a. To capture France with a swift attack

85.   d. Six weeks

86.   a. The Battle of the Marne

87.   a. Erich von Falkenhayn

88.   a. Liege

89.   d. Austria-Hungary

90.   a. The Schlieffen Plan

91.   a. He increased the military's size and strength

92.   a. January 4, 1913

93.   a. Paris

94.   c. Blitzkrieg

95.   d. Six weeks

96.   a. He assessed the situation and ordered a retreat

97.   c. Gerhard Ritter

98.   d. Both a and c

99.   d. There was no code name

100.   c. 20 percent

Race to the Sea

101.   b. To outflank and encircle German troops in France and Belgium

102.   d. Neither side won

103.   d. All the above

104.   c. November 22, 1914

105.   d. All the above

106.   b. North Sea

107.   b. 350-400 miles

108.   b. 1914

109.   d. They set up a defensive line on the north coast

110.   a. A trench warfare stalemate

111.   a. First stage

112.   d. Outflanking and encircling Allied troops in France and Belgium

113.   d. They set up defensive lines on the English Channel coast

114.   d. Belgian forces

115.   b. October 12,1914

116.   c. Dig trenches and fortify their positions

117.   c. Allied Powers and Central Powers

118.   d. All the above

119.   b. First Battle of Ypres

120.   c. The First Battle of the Marne

Trench Warfare and Battles on the Western Front

121.   a. To create an impregnable defensive line to protect France and Great Britain

122.   c. Ten months

123.   d. Marne River Valley

124.   d. Canada

125.   a. Field Marshal Douglas Haig

126.   b. Trench warfare

127.   a. July 31, 1917

128.   d. 440 miles

129.   b. The Second Battle of Ypres

130.   c. French forces emerged victorious and forced German troops to retreat

131.   b. Food shortages

132.   d. All the above

133.   a. April 1915

134.   d. United States

135.   b. Tanks

136.   a. 300 days

137.   d. The invasion of Normandy

138.   d. 1918

139.   b. Second Battle of Ypres

140.   c. "Over There"

Eastern Front Battles and Strategies

141.   d. Siege of Przemysl

142.   a. 1915

143.   a. Treaties of Brest-Litovsk

144.   a. To avoid encirclement, shorten the front lines, and buy time to resupply

145.   a. Voluntarily declared war

146.   b. St. Petersburg, which was changed to Petrograd

147.   a. Austria-Hungary, Bulgaria, and Turkey

148.   b. Poland

149.   a. Lack of ammunition/munitions

150.   a. Allied forces attempted to intervene in Russian affairs

151.   b. Two days

152.   a. Grigori Rasputin

153.   b. Union of Zemstvos and Municipalities

154.   d. The Twentieth Siberian Rifle Regiment

155.   c. General Aleksei Brusilov

156.   a. With a swift counterattack

157.   b. Ukraine and Russia

158.   c. To relieve pressure on the Western Front

159.   b. 1915

160.   a. They launched a counteroffensive

Balkans Theatre

161. a. Eastern Front
162. a. 1914
163. d. Battle of Cer
164. b. General Oskar Potiorek
165. a. The fall of Belgrade
166. a. Nellie Bly
167. a. The Salonika Campaign
168. a. The 1918 Treaty of Bucharest
169. b. 1915
170. a. Greece
171. d. 1917
172. a. 1918
173. c. Eleftherios Venizelos
174. a. The 1917 Battle of Monastir
175. a. Russia
176. c. 1914
177. b. Battle of Sellenberk
178. b. Jihad
179. a. Austria-Hungary and the Ottoman Empire
180. c. Battle of Transylvania

Naval Warfare (Battle of Jutland)

181. c. 1916
182. a. British and German navies
183. a. North Sea
184. d. Battleships
185. a. The ammunition magazines
186. a. 10,000
187. a. Great Britain
188. c. Both sides claimed victory
189. b. Admiral John Jellicoe

190. b. Admiral Reinhard Scheer

191. a. Twenty-five

192. a. Battle of Skagerrak

193. b. Great Britain

194. c. In Denmark and northern Germany

195. d. Both a and c

196. b. A Germanic tribe called the "Jutes"

197. b. Iron Dog

198. d. 250 warships

199. a. *Battleship*

200. d. Over twenty-four hours

The Russian Revolution

201. c. 1917

202. b. Bolshevik Party

203. c. Formation of workers' councils

204. a. Trotsky

205. a. Russia's participation in WWI

206. a. Nicholas II

207. a. Each other in a civil war

208. c. October 1917

209. b. Mensheviks

210. d. Petrograd Uprising

211. c. He largely ignored and then repressed them

212. a. Alexander Kerensky

213. a. St. Petersburg (Petrograd)

214. b. Mensheviks

215. d. Bolshevik Coup (October Revolution)

216. c. Private ownership of industry

217. c. Felix Yusupov

218. d. Enthusiastic and patriotic

219. d. 1921–1922

220. d. Robbing banks

American Entry into the War

221.   d. 1917

222.   a. He declared neutrality for the United States

223.   a. France, Russia, Britain, and Italy

224.   a. By attacking US merchant vessels carrying supplies to Allied forces

225.   c. He demanded the Germans stop targeting passenger ships and threatened to cut diplomatic ties

226.   a. To protect America's interests and restore peace and freedom throughout Europe

227.   c. The Zimmerman Telegram

228.   c. He did not respond, maintaining neutrality for the United States

229.   d. Joint resolution authorizing US participation in WWI

230.   a. Money and supplies

231.   a. Five million

232.   a. General John J. Pershing

233.   d. Refusal to compromise with the Senate to ensure US membership in the League of Nations

234.   d. To create lasting peace and stability throughout Europe

235.   d. December 7, 1917

236.   a. George M. Cohan

237.   b. To provide support for Allied forces on the front lines

238.   c. He kept us out of the war!

239.   d. To establish a lasting peace and stability throughout Europe

240.   b. Robert Lansing

Armistice Agreement

241.   c. November 11, 1918

242.   d. All the above

243.   d. Netherlands

244.   c. An end to active hostilities

245.   a. German troops stopped fighting

246.   a. Fulfillment of Wilson's pledge to make the world safe for democracy

247.   a. Marshal Ferdinand Foch

248.   d. A cessation of hostilities and withdrawal from occupied territory

249.   d. Both a and b

250.   a. War would erupt again in twenty years

251.   c. Paris, France

252.   c. The League of Nations

253.   a. They would be released immediately

254.   d. Marshal Foch

255.   c. German troops

256.   a. Russia

257.   d. All the above

258.   d. Recovering in a military hospital

259.   c. Eighteen

260.   a. Marshal Foch

Treaty of Versailles

261.   b. Hermann Müller and Johannes Bell

262.   c. 132 billion gold marks

263.   b. League of Nations

264.   c. Section V

265.   b. Article 231

266.   b. The Mandate System

267.   b. January 10, 1920

268.   d. 2010

269.   a. It was unnecessarily punitive and unfairly placed too much blame on Germany

270.   b. Allied recognition that Germany does not have the money to pay all reparations

271.   a. The War Guilt Clause

272.   a. German possessions in China and the Pacific

273.   b. Italians felt that they did not receive enough territorial gains

274.   b. Georges Clemenceau

275.   d. United States

276.   a. Germany was required to maintain an army of no greater than 100,000 soldiers

277.   b. Because of political opposition to the League of Nations

278.   a. The Weimar Republic

279.   b. Germany was forced to cede territories in Europe and Asia

280.   d. The Treaty imposed heavy financial reparation payments that crippled its economy

Technology Used in WWI

281.   d. 1917

282.   d. Both a and b

283.   c. Gotha bomber

284.   c. Ernest Swinton

285.   c. For bombing missions

286.   a. Sopwith Camel

287.   a. SPAD XIII fighter plane

288.   a. Offensively against enemy troops

289.   a. Germany

290.   c. Ernest Swinton

291.   d. 230

292.   b. Fokker Eindecker

293.   a. Germany

294.   d. All the above

295.   c. A7V Sturmpanzerwagen

296.   b. Fritz Haber

297.   d. All the above

298.   b. Ferdinand von Zeppelin

299.   a. Sopwith Camel

300.   c. Rangefinders

Propaganda in WWI

301. d. All the above
302. a. Posters, speeches, newspapers, and pamphlets
303. d. All the above
304. d. Alfred Leete
305. a. France
306. b. Anarchists
307. a. Edward Bernays
308. d. All the above
309. d. All the above
310. a. Huns
311. b. France and the United States
312. d. All the above
313. d. All the above
314. a. Norman Angell
315. a. Herbert Asquith
316. b. Erich Maria Remarque
317. d. All the above
318. a. "God punish England!"
319. a. "Your Country Needs You" poster
320. b. Remember Belgium

Home Fronts During WWI

321. a. The expansion of segregation in the United States
322. d. Write and receive letters
323. b. Food control
324. b. United States
325. b. Food Will Win the War campaign
326. a. To provide fresh produce for civilians while freeing up commercial produce for soldiers
327. a. Two million
328. d. All the above
329. d. Increased taxes and improved military preparedness

330.	c. Erich Ludendorff
331.	a. War Industries Board
332.	a. Food, metal, rubber, and textiles
333.	b. Agriculture
334.	d. All the above
335.	b. Women's Land Army
336.	b. 1916
337.	d. All the above
338.	a. U.S. Food Administration
339.	a. The U.S. Food Administration
340.	b. Liberty loan campaign

U-Boat Campaigns and Blockades

341.	d. All the above
342.	b. Great Britain
343.	d. Germany
344.	a. February 1915
345.	c. In the Baltic
346.	c. Increased diplomatic tension with the United States
347.	a. Submarines
348.	b. To disrupt Allied supply lines
349.	a. Kaiser Wilhelm II
350.	d. It deployed minesweepers throughout European waters
351.	b. 375
352.	d. All the above
353.	c. By attacking merchant ships without warning
354.	c. 1917
355.	c. Torpedo attacks from underwater
356.	b. It led to food shortages
357.	b. 6,000
358.	b. Germany lost its naval advantage
359.	d. Submarine tenders
360.	a. Britain

British Empire's Contributions

361. d. India

362. c. Battle of Kut

363. c. Mahatma Gandhi

364. b. The Indian Corps

365. c. Canada

366. a. Two billion dollars

367. a. Victoria Cross

368. c. 1914

369. c. Indian Expeditionary Force

370. d. 37

371. c. Lawrence Binyon

372. d. Australia

373. d. Australia

374. b. Canada

375. a. 1914

376. a. One hundred million pounds

377. d. The Indian National Volunteer Corp

378. d. Australia and New Zealand Army Corps

379. a. Battle of Passchendaele

380. d. The United States

Creation of the League of Nations

381. c. 1920

382. b. To prevent further wars and promote international cooperation

383. a. Woodrow Wilson

384. d. 42

385. b. Woodrow Wilson

386. c. Sir Eric Drummond

387. c. The Assembly

388. a. Germany, Russia, and Austria-Hungary

389. a. One vote

390.   a. The Council

391.   a. Member nation contributions

392.   a. United States

393.   b. It monitored territories mandated by the league after WWI

394.   d. Japan and China

395.   a. Economic and Financial Organisation

396.   d. All the above

397.   b. Fifty-eight

398.   a. Woodrow Wilson

399.   a. Establishing international law governing how minorities should be treated

400.   a. It officially dissolved in 1946

Post-War Economic Crisis and Inflationary Pressures

401.   a. It was forced to pay reparations that caused its currency to collapse

402.   c. It caused wages to remain stagnant while prices rose rapidly

403.   c. 1923

404.   d. Britain

405.   a. Nearly 100 percent

406.   d Austria faced inflation and economic depression

407.   c. Both a and b

408.   d. Increased debt and printing of money

409.   d. All the above

410.   c. Both a and b

411.   a. Implementing austerity measures such as budget cuts

412.   d. Global economic decline

413.   c. Both a and b

414.   d. All the above

415.   d. Increased investment opportunities

416.   d. Consumers can buy less with same amount of money

417.   b. Germany

418.   a. It radicalized them

419.   d. All the above

420.   d. Cheap drinks and the political discourse of beer halls became more popular (Consider the Beer Hall Putsch)

Impact on Civilian Populations

421.   a. Increased poverty and hardship

422.   b. It caused a military draft among young men, leading to decreased labor availability

423.   d. All the above

424.   d. It increased overcrowding among troops and civilians

425.   d. All the above

426.   b. Reduced access to staple goods such as food and fuel

427.   d. All the above

428.   d. Both a and c

429.   d. Diverting manpower into the military, leaving fewer adults available for work

430.   c. By forcing soldiers away from their families and creating a demand for sexual services

431.   d. All the above

432.   d. Decreasing family size as men were away at war and women had to take on more responsibilities

433.   a. By diverting resources away from schools to military endeavors

434.   a. By creating the need for people to flee violence and war-torn regions

435.   a. Increased mortality rates due to disease and malnutrition

436.   d. Both a and b

437.   d. All the above

438.   d. Both b and c

439.   d. All the above

440.   a. 6-13 million

Role of Women During WWI

441.   a. Denmark

442.   b. Columbia

443.   c. 1917

444.   a. Zero

445.   a. The Red Cross

446.   b. 1917

447.   a. Factory work

448.   a. 18

449.   b.1917

450.   c. *The Schemes of the Kaiser*

451.   a. 100

452.   a. Opha May Johnson

453.   b. Medical support

454.   b. United Kingdom

455.   b. Princess Evgeniya Shakhovskaya

456.   c. 40 percent

457.   c. 1918

458.   c. The Women's Social and Political Union

459.   b. Over 10,000

460.   c. Clara Immerwahr

Colonialism, Aftermath, and New National Borders

461.   c. Serbia

462.   b. Ethiopia

463.   d. Treaty of Versailles

464.   b. Germany

465.   a. There was an increased push toward self-determination and independence

466.   c. By issuing mandates for territories formerly controlled by defeated powers

467.   d. 1932

468.   d. Indian Independence Act

469.   a. Sykes-Picot Agreement

470.   b. They were to become independent countries

471.   c. 1922

472.   d. Tanganyika, Togoland, and Cameroon

473.   c. 1922

474.   d. All the above

475.   a. Five

476.   b. Greece

477.   d. Turkey

478.   c. 1922

479.   c. By issuing mandates for territories formerly controlled by defeated powers

480.   d. Japan and Britan (through Australia/New Zealand)

Medical Advances, Intelligence Gathering, and Espionage during WWI

481.   c. Codebreaking

482.   d. Two hours

483.   a. Wilhelm Röntgen

484.   a. Artillery and anti-aircraft fire control

485.   b. Motorized ambulance transport

486.   b. 1915

487.   c. Anne Morgan

488.   a. Carl Hans Lody

489.   b. Sonar

490.   a. John Scott Haldane

491.   a. Room 40

492.   d. All the above

493.   c. Tanks

494.   b. Fear of espionage

495.   a. Skin grafts

496.   a. Radio

497.   a. Through the use of "signals intelligence"
498.   a. Trench foot
499.   b. A mechanical hand
500.   b. Zeppelins

Check out another book in the series

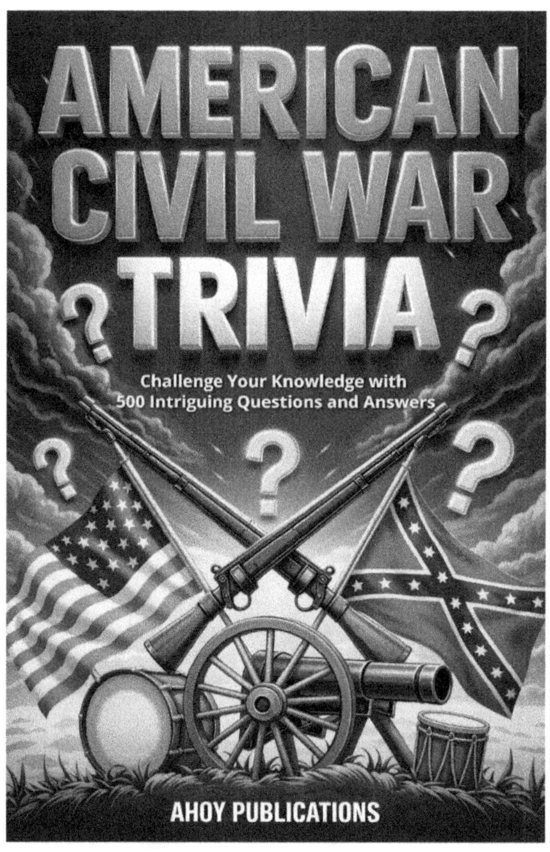

Welcome Aboard, Check Out This Limited-Time Free Bonus!

Ahoy, reader! Welcome to the Ahoy Publications family, and thanks for snagging a copy of this book! Since you've chosen to join us on this journey, we'd like to offer you something special.

Check out the link below for a FREE e-book filled with delightful facts about American History.

But that's not all - you'll also have access to our exclusive email list with even more free e-books and insider knowledge. Well, what are ye waiting for? Click the link below to join and set sail toward exciting adventures in American History.

Access your bonus here

https://ahoypublications.com/

Or, Scan the QR code!